Mindfulness in a Time of Grief

Cheryl Muck

Mindfulness In A Time Of Grief

Published By Cheryl Muck
1st edition Published March 2021

Photography with digital Waterlogue app:
Cheryl Muck
Michael Smith
Book and cover Design:
Richard K. McNeill

Library of Congress Control Number: 2020916611
ISBN: 978-0-578-75196-2

Printed in The USA

Dedication

Dedicated to all those
Lost to COVID 19
in a time of great sorrow.

May their legacy
profoundly change how we relate
one with another.

May humanity come together
knowing that we are each dependent
one with another.

Photo: Cheryl Muck

• • •

Table of Contents

You can find practices on my YouTube channel. Look for this symbol:

[illegible]

Photo: Cheryl Muck

Come join me in my courtyard.
Take a moment right now.
Close your eyes and breath slowly
and deeply.
Feel the calm center which is
always available in your heart.

PREFACE: July 2019

I believe life is full of synchronicity. Some call it luck or coincidence or destiny or fate. Whatever it is called, I have tried to pay attention when life throws those synchronicities onto my path. In the early 1970's, I was lucky enough to attend an extraordinarily progressive nursing school at Fort Hays State University in Hays, Kansas. For various personal reasons, I became fascinated with Elizabeth Kubler-Ross's research and 1969 book *On Death and Dying*. Her research and writings started a revolution that continues to impact how the medical community understands and cares for the terminally ill. In my undergraduate program, I completed a special study project on death and dying. I then completed my Masters in Nursing at Texas Woman's University. My studies focused on home health, gerontology, terminal illness, grief and end of life.

My first leadership job was with the Visiting Nurse Association of Dallas, the second largest home care company in the USA at that time. In the late 1970's, the VNA of Dallas was selected by the Federal Government to be one of the Demonstration Research Project sites to evaluate and support the development and payment for Hospice in the United States. I was one of the VNA managers responsible for implementing and collecting research data for that government project. The project provided us with a unique opportunity to comment on and impact government decisions regarding Hospice services, delivery methods and payment systems. Based on that research, Congress created the Medicare Hospice Benefit in 1982. The rest of my home health nursing career was interwoven with hospice.

Working with hospice patients/families, staff and volunteers changes how one sees the world. The best of who I am comes from my hospice encounters and the wisdom of folks facing mortality. Those encounters have informed my own personal response to life, loss and grief through the years. I offer this book to honor their lives.

What I have written here comes through me but is really from all those who have shared their experiences with me. May the blessings they have brought to my life also touch yours.

Now you have a little context of who I am and why I wrote this book. I don't have all the answers, and I certainly can't make your pain go away. But this I know for sure, you already have everything that you need to live through your loss. May this book shine a light on your path.

If you are reading this book, grief has touched your life. I am imagining you as I sit at my computer. My heart fills with compassion and loving-kindness for you. This book is offered to support you on your individual healing journey. Your grief is your own and very personal. Yet, it is also one with all of humanity's grief. We are all on the path of grief recovery. We each have a heart that aches from the losses and suffering this world brings. As you grieve the world grieves with you. As the world grieves, we all grieve together.

May you learn to gently hold your grief in awareness and to mindfully watch your healing progress. Allow yourself to learn and grow from your loss at your own pace. Although it might feel abnormal or painful at first, try being consciously aware of your grief. You can learn to support your healing with love and compassion. You can hold yourself with self-compassion every day. The decision to avoid or delay the pain until you are ready or have time may actually be your current truth, or it may simply delay your process, only you know the answer. Most of us aren't very good at taking care of ourselves. Sometimes we even falsely believe it is selfish to do so. The truth is that when you care for yourself first, you also help others - especially during grief.

Come join me in my courtyard.
Take a moment right now.
Close your eyes and breath slowly and deeply.
Feel the calm center which is always available in your heart.

Together let us become more mindful of our common and individual suffering. Let us allow the broken heart to begin to mend. Let us breathe in healing. Let the pain escape with each out breath. I feel you there. May you feel and receive compassion, healing and loving-kindness.

There are no magic pills or secret remedies to resolve the pain of grief. However, I assure you that there is a vast wholeness and a deep strength already available and waiting for you. May the practices found in this book help you tap into that eternal energy, however you choose to name it.

You are safe

You are loved

You are free

Congratulations, you are taking actions to be mindful of your grief, the first step to consciously moving through your recovery. The grief path is painful whether it is walked in a mindless or a mindful way. Life moves forward either way. May your grief recovery road be blessed with mindful awareness, self-compassion, loving-kindness, and may you once again find joy!

Cheryl Muck
July 2019

Photo: Cheryl Muck

PREFACE: July 2020

This book was started in 2018, and finished in 2020, just before the start of the COVID 19 pandemic. I wrote this book as an offering to help those suffering from the typical loss and grief experienced in each life. I never suspected the world was on the cusp of a worldwide time of great sorrow. I never expected the world to change so quickly. I never dreamed that suffering would become a world-wide shared experience.

I am humbled by the strength, service and loving-kindness the entire world has shown during this pandemic. As a whole, humanity has responded with compassion, sacrifice and community effort in a way never seen before. Most have put human life and health above normalcy and wealth. To protect the population at risk of death from COVID 19, entire nations have changed the very fabric of society in the blink of an eye. Individuals, communities, nations, and the world are forever changed. It is certainly too early to know if these changes will ultimately be for the better. I tend to believe that all things work together for good, so I am viewing these painful events with a hopeful heart for humanity.

As in all times of great anguish and pain, there is also much that is good. Families are eating together and talking to one another. Communities are supporting each other and consciously celebrating the helpers in their communities. Technology advances are allowing us to come together without being physically present.

On a grander scale, there are some positive changes. We can visualize our planet's amazing ability to heal herself. Look to Los Angeles or the Himalayas where air quality improved beyond expectation after just 30 days of human lock-down in response to the pandemic. Scientists around the world are working in cooperation to develop medical treatments and vaccines. There is a growing awareness that we have more in common than we previously had thought. We have a heightened awareness of our interdependence as both nations and individuals. People of all races are coming together to say we stand united in our desire for equality for all.

This book was not written for the pandemic. Yet it speaks to the heart of what we are feeling. With our ability to quickly communicate worldwide, this may be the first time in human history that the entire world is suffering through a collective experience. Loss and grief come in many forms, but here and now there is shared loss and grief. Our suffering is both an individual experience and a common-to-all crisis.

The human spirit is always changed by profound loss and grief. May we stay mindful of our loss and sorrow. May we use our grief to change in positive ways. May our hearts be broken open and expand to hold every being in reverence. May we gain insights regarding our common humanity. May we grow in wisdom. May we behave with loving-kindness. May compassion direct our actions.

Stay safe. Live peace. Share joy.

Namaste - that which is Holy in me greets that which is Holy in you,
Cheryl Muck
July 2020

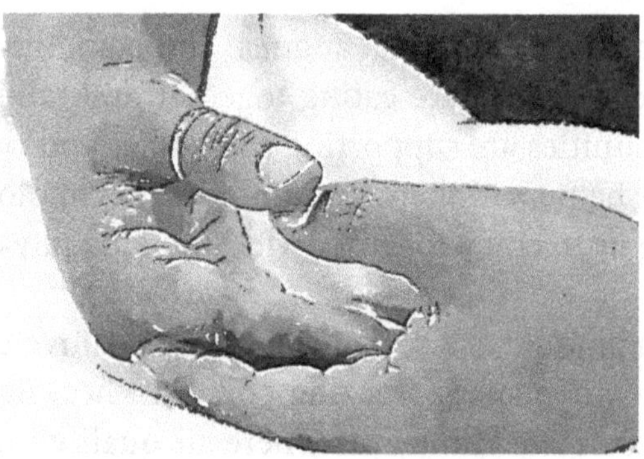

Photo: Courtesy Dallas Meditation Center

Photo: Michael Smith

Releasing Expectations

An action poem: sit, visualize, experience the peace which passes all understanding

Breathing in
    Healing compassion
Breathing out
    Releasing fear

Breathing in
    Healing grace
Breathing out
    Releasing guilt

Breathing in
    Healing acceptance
Breathing out
    Releasing expectations

Breathing in
    Healing joy
Breathing out
    Releasing grief

Introduction

It is easy to get stuck in the pain of grief and loss. It is tempting to hold onto the past and the way things were before. Sometimes we believe moving on is unfair when someone is gone. Practicing self-care can help resolve this suffering. Learn to identify when you are mired down in loss and then consciously take the path that helps heal your grief. It takes courage to experience loss, to be present with it, and to then move forward. Healing loss and grief is supported by staying mindful and practicing self-care every day. You have suffered an incredible loss, so show yourself the same patience and kindness you would show your best friend. This book found its way into your life to support another chapter of your journey, and it is an invitation to take an active role in healing your grief.

All you need to heal yourself is already within you. Take time to find your own strength and truth. Give yourself permission to do what works for you! As long as it does not harm you or another, do whatever it takes to heal, move forward and live a joy-filled life. Each day lived mindfully decreases suffering and fosters joy. Breathe in life and acceptance. Breathe out pain and release fear. Mindfully experience your loss. Grieve for your loss. But also allow happiness to flow in. Allow yourself to experience the joy of life again. You can hold onto loving memories and also feel joy. Your heart and soul are big enough to hold the memories and the losses while continuing to experience the joy of living each moment.

This book provides proven techniques which can help you harness painful emotions to create insights. You will learn how to calm the body and focus the mind using breathing exercises which support a natural self-healing loop. You will observe that being present in the moment provides an honest connection to reality. You will experience the joy of living in the moment, as well as a peace not available in thoughts of the past or visions of the future. You will discover resiliency, compassion, courage, and maybe even joy as you strengthen your ability to identify and acknowledge emotions without judgement. You will develop the strength to be with your loss, to experience it, to grow from it. This book will ask you:

- To be mindfully present with your grief.
- To accept your emotions without judgement.
- To allow grief to be as it is without trying to change it.
- To use your breath to calm your body when feeling overwhelmed.
- To embrace growth and change as a natural outcome of the grief experience.

Learning how to use mindfulness as a healing tool

Let us start with what mindfulness is not. Mindfulness does not require you to have any specific belief system or faith background. Mindfulness can support any faith or religion. Mindfulness does not require you to stop your thoughts, although it may result in a quieter mind. Although mindfulness is not meditation or yoga, although meditation and yoga both support becoming more mindful. Mindfulness is not difficult. Everyone already experiences moments of mindfulness, we can all learn to be more mindful.

Mindfulness is simply the act of being present in each moment without judgement or expectations. Increasing mindfulness transforms grief and is a skill that anyone can learn. It is a simple process, but it requires practice. Anyone can increase their ability to be mindful. In fact, we are all mindful at least from time to time.

Think about the first time you fell in love. One of the glories of that experience is the acute awareness and overwhelming focus on the other without judgement. All the senses light up, and we become acutely aware and focused on every moment. We are enthralled with the smallest event. We all remember that feeling of joy and wonder. That is mindfulness.

Consider a time when you were involved with a favorite hobby or activity. It captured your complete thoughts. You were actively engaged in the creative activity and totally focused on the present moment. The past and future did not exist, only this glorious moment and activity. You were fully engrossed. There was no judgement or analysis. There was just the doing. There was just the being. There was just the sheer joy of living in the moment! That is mindfulness.

Mindfulness also occurs in difficult times. In very difficult or traumatic times, our senses become acute and our focus sharpens. Over time the mind may twist the facts and distort the traumatic memory, but our body remembers the feelings with clarity. Events become seared into our minds, like the break up with our first love, the death of our first pet, a near death experience, the loss of a parent — any time we become acutely aware of the current moment— That is mindfulness.

Mindfulness will not make your grief go away. However, it can provide a foundation for healing. Consciously dealing with your grief will help you learn to navigate a new loss-filled reality. When we remain present with our grief and pain we support healing and transformation. Some losses are so great we begin to see life as before or after our loss. We may believe we will never be whole again. Mindfulness can help us recognize when our mind is trapped in the illusion of an incomplete and divided life. Without judgement, we can learn to gently return to the present moment, which is truly all we ever have. We can learn to face our loss and pain in the present moment with self-compassion. As we become more mindful, it becomes easier to use our breath to calm the body and focus the mind. Learning to be present with grief, as it arises, will gradually decrease the frequency of unexpected and overwhelming grief episodes. That is mindfulness in a time of grief.

There are learnable practices that increase mindfulness. We can use our breath to calm our body and rest our mind. We can practice meditation which leads to mindfulness. We can use prayer to connect to the holiness of every moment. We can actively engage in a creative activity which keeps us focused on the present moment and we can pause every time we are stressed and gently return to the present moment without judgement, thus opening ourselves to a more mindful state.

Use the practices found in this book to support your grief recovery. Over the next two or three months you will establish the habit of living mindfully to support your grief process. This book provides resources to help you be present with your grief and continue with your life.

Summary of Book Contents

Chapter 1: SUPPORTING GROWTH: Understanding how to support positive change

This chapter creates the foundation for seeing grief as a natural process to deal with loss. It briefly outlines the science of positive change. It will review how to foster positive thinking, make healthy choices, recognize and stop unhelpful thoughts, use positive affirmations and establish constructive habits.

Chapter 2: BREATHING PRACTICES: Taking action to calm the body

This chapter reviews how the breath can naturally calm the body when you are overwhelmed with emotion or pain. It also provides specific breathing practices to support your grief process. These breathing practices are simple to learn but can change your life. Try them all and then use the ones that work best for you.

Chapter 3: DOING THE WORK: Practices to support healing

This chapter is the meat of the book. Reading and thinking about grief are merely mental exercises, whereas moving through grief requires personal awareness and action. These exercises are offered as a tool to help you do the work of grieving. Use these practice sessions routinely to support your healing journey and to stimulate your own personal healing activities.

This chapter may help you learn new skills or brush up on some previously used ones. The changes you make are your choice. My hope is that this book will in some small way help you honor that which you have lost. May it also help you support yourself with compassion and love. As we grow in self-compassion and self-love, our ability to share love and compassion grows.

Read and contemplate

Each practice session has a reading to encourage a period of quiet contemplation. Contemplation allows us to be present with our grief. You may find that giving yourself time to practice self-healing on a daily basis helps you move through the grief process with greater ease. We all must process our loss and related grief.

Take action

Each practice session includes concrete action items that can help you heal. The practice exercises have been recorded and can be found on my YouTube channel. Listening to the exercises may work better than reading them. For many people, it is easier to learn and practice the skills while listening. Reading uses a part of the brain that may make it harder to relax and practice at the same time.

- Breathing break: The action exercise starts with a breath practice to calm your body and mind. Consciously stopping for a breathing break is a wonderful gift you can give yourself.

- Action exercise: These encourage you to take time to be present with your feelings. They are designed to help you take positive actions which will support your healing.

- Breathing break: It is suggested that you then close the practice session with another calming breath practice. This will allow you to once again consciously calm your body and mind before returning to the difficulties of your life.

Practice healing in your daily life

Each practice session concludes with a Positive Affirmation. I invite you to carry the positive affirmations into your daily life. On a daily basis use the positive affirmation as a reminder that you choose to do the work of healing. If the affirmation is one with which you struggle, you may elect to use it over a longer period of time.

Final Sections

The Moving Forward section will help you consider your growth and how to continue the work of grief and life. It will encourage you to embrace change and loss as a normal part of the cycle of life.

The book concludes with Suggested Resources. It outlines some of my most loved books, websites and resources. They have informed my life and stretched my mind to new dimensions. Many of the thoughts and concepts in this book originated from reading and contemplating on those materials. I may have watered and tended the thought, but those writers planted the seed. You may choose to investigate them as you continue on your own life journey.

Photo: Cheryl Muck

Photo: Cheryl Muck

CHAPTER 1 CREATING POSITIVE CHANGE:

Understanding how to support positive growth

This chapter was written for those interested in some of the basic science behind the methods and techniques suggested in this book. It provides a general overview of related knowledge-based techniques. It also provides enough information to support further investigation of those methods that you find helpful.

There is an abundance of research and knowledge which can support us in our healing and growth and change. (See the section on Suggested Resources at the end of the book, if you want more detailed information). The concepts and suggestions reviewed in this chapter may prove helpful as you go through the grief process. However, it isn't necessary to understand the scientific principles or research for the techniques to work.

I invite you to read this chapter whenever you feel it works best for you. If you are in an emotionally charged stage of loss and grief, the information may seem overwhelming and too detailed to deal with right now. If your loss is very recent, you may choose to skip this section for now and return to it later when the intensity of your pain decreases. In the beginning of your grief, it may be hard to focus. During the most intense stages of grief, it is best to focus on simply being present in the moment, breathing and healing. Chapter 3 will better support you in that effort. There are three topics which are directly tied to the practices found in Chapter 3. If you want, you may decide to read them now - 'Establish Constructive Habits' (page 21), 'Breathing Practices' (Chapter 2, page 25), and 'Use Positive Affirmations' (page 18).

When the time is right and you are ready to move forward, review this Chapter to better understand some of these techniques. Use the information that helps you become stronger and move through your loss and grief. Everyone is different. Some of these concepts may be new to you, and some will probably be information you already know. Take what resonates and apply it in your life.

Foster positive thinking

Positive thinking helps with stress management and strengthens our health. Most of us have a tendency to predominantly think in either positive or negative ways. You know if you are a half-full or half-empty glass kind of person. If you are lucky enough to be a positive thinker, it may be easier to approach loss and grief in a more positive way. If you are a negative thinker, you may find loss and grief more challenging. There are things you can do to increase positive thinking during this time. These are all great skills to have in your good-life tool box. Here are some suggested actions that gradually increase positive thinking.

Meditation practice

Reading a book is only a mental exercise. While reading and thinking may lead to some insight, it does not bring the same personal gains as practicing meditation and living mindfully. That applies to this book as well as to all the others out there! Mindfulness and meditation are about the experience, the doing and the being. They are only words until we do the work and actually practice the behaviors. Meditation and mindfulness are called a practice because we always strive to grow and become more skilled. It is a learn-as-you-go activity. These practices are not about a religious or spiritual point of view; these practices are complementary to all religions and philosophies of life.

One of the best ways to develop clarity of mind and a more positive outlook is to live a more mindful life. If our mind is engaged with something in the present moment, it is typically based more firmly in logic, reason, and reality. Mindfulness keeps our brains engaged and productive, thus decreasing the room for useless chatter and negativity.

You may think meditating requires too much time. Folks that routinely meditate will say that their practice actually saves them time and makes their life more meaningful and happy. For those new to meditation, it may be helpful to use a meditation application. My favorites are *Calm* and *Headspace*; they are readily available for purchase in any application store. Once you are comfortable with the process, it can easily be practiced independently without using an app.

Practice at least 15 minutes of meditation faithfully every day for 66 days. Within that time frame most people begin to experience positive results which continue to grow over time. It is also helpful to develop a support group. The energy of group meditation is very powerful. A weekly group meditation will amplify your personal results. An internet search will help you find local meditation groups.

Understand your chatter-box

Positive thinking is significantly tied to self-talk. I call this the chatter-box, and we all have one. It is that little voice of unspoken thoughts that fill our minds. While some of this chatter is based on logic, reason, and reality, much of it is not valuable. This chatter is filler for the mind as it takes in, synthesizes and categorizes information. When the mind is not busy with important stuff it may tend to lecture. The mind is always working, and it even makes up problems to solve while lecturing us! Spend some time rationally listening to your own chatter-box. If it says things to you that you would never dream of saying to another person, you have a mean chatter-box. Some of us have really nasty chatter-boxes.

The chatter-box nearly always focuses on the past or on the future. That is a trick the mind uses to keep itself busy. If there is nothing of interest going on right now, the mind tends to go around and around on the same issue, ruminating like a cow chewing its cud. This can cause negativity or depression. Instead, try to stay mindfully focused on what is going on right now. Learn to identify when your mind is playing a time trick on you and, then consciously come back to this moment. The ability to recognize and call out your own mind when it is misbehaving will create a positive shift in your thoughts. This is a foreign concept to most of us. You may believe you have no control over your mind. That is a false belief generated by your own mind!

Once you understand that you have control over your own mind, life becomes amazingly better. Try to routinely question your own mind! When your mind is going around and around worried about something in the past or future, stop and exam the issues logically. Would you believe it if someone else was saying it? Is the thought based on sure facts or is the thought based on fears, insecurities and anxieties? There is amazing freedom in not believing every thought that pops into the head. With a little practice, even your own mind will agree that some thoughts are just not accurate and should not be believed.

Identify and spend time with people that build you up

During your grief process actively identify and spend time with those people that provide a healthy environment for healing. Seek out the most positive people in each segment of your life family, personal, work, church, social, etc. Some people may increase your stress and pain especially during loss and grief. As much as possible, isolate yourself from those people that have a negative impact on you.

Relationships are much like construction sites. They are always in the process of tearing down, sitting idle, or building up. Most of us don't want to be torn down. Sitting idle for short periods of time can create clarity and new vision, but in the long run no progress is made. On the other hand, we can all take some building up and improving. So, choose friends that build you up. Fostering and growing the right relationships make a major difference in one's life. Our friends may be the best predictor of who we will be in the next 5 to 10 years.

Take some time to honestly evaluate your current relationships. Do you have friends and family that are there for you? Do you have those for whom you would be there when needed? It takes time to develop strong, positive and supportive relationships. Even though we cannot always select family and work peers, we do get to choose our friends. Take advantage of that fact and choose your friends wisely. It will change your life.

For the most part, our friends and even our family are similar to who we are. Our best friends usually have some common interests, values and goals. Friends also typically see the world through many of the same filters as we do. This brings comfort and familiarity. However, diversity in friends and family may help one see and learn things not easily seen through our own filters. For example, if you lose a spouse early and your friends are mostly the same age as you, it may be difficult for them to relate to your experience.

When we lose someone, it can be tempting to close down and hold people at a distance. You may not feel like going out to seek new friends or relationships but try to be open to people that reach out. It is healing to spend time with those that bring us comfort and make us feel safe. It is also beneficial to expand and diversify friends to get a broader view of life. Allow yourself the freedom to be open to new friends.

It may be helpful to spend a little time thinking about your current relationships. Consider what characteristics make people special in your life. Make it a practice to spend more time with the folks that bring light, comfort and joy into your life. If you can, tell them why they are special to you. Everyone loves to hear why they are special.

Consider making a list of characteristics you value in a relationship. One size does not fit all; there are no right or wrong special characteristics. When you think about and make your own list, remember no friend is going to meet all your needs. We may have one friend that lifts us up and encourages our growth, and another that accepts us just as we are without judgment. One friend may be our good time buddy, and another may be there when we are down. If you are lucky, you will find some friends that serve more than one of the characteristics you value.

Develop your own list; you know best what you need in a friend or loving family member. I personally value the following characteristics. Maybe this list will help your creative juices flow.

- **Positive outlook on life.** I feel uplifted and energized when I am around positive people; and afterwards the feeling persists. When I spend time with them, I feel strong, capable and happy. Although they are usually fun to be around, this doesn't mean they are always happy and cheerful. The key is they make me feel happy and positive about life in general, and happiness is contagious.
- **Honesty.** Having an honest conversation with a friend makes my heart sing. It is liberating. I find it helpful to get honest feedback as long as it is done with loving-kindness and/or humor. I need to feel heard and understood but not judged.
- **Critical thinking skills.** Friends with critical thinking skills are always able to step out of their own world view, review a situation, and provide insight with helpful advice. Critical thinkers have lots of curiosity, want to learn more and are open to new ideas. They are skeptical, want to question everything, and require evidence to believe something. Critical thinkers are willing to humbly change their opinion when faced with new evidence that supports another view.
- **Supportive.** A friend's support helps me feel safe and encourages me to grow into my own best self. I think it is helpful to have friends that balance my skills and weaknesses so that we can help each other grow and learn. I highly value knowledge and growth, so I enjoy friends that support that part of me. It is a plus if they have the capability to challenge and motivate me.
- **Reliability.** Like most others, I need friends that are routinely

present in my life and always there for me when I need them. There are so many ways to stay in contact today. We do not have to be physically in contact to stay connected. New and intermediate relationships can mature when given time and attention. Long term relationships continually require time and commitment to maintain a strong bond.

- **Similar interests.** Friendships typically develop based on shared interests. I have a variety of interests and value diversity so my friend groups reflect my personal interests. As a result, I have friends that rarely cross paths but know and hear about each other.

Photo: Cheryl Muck

Make healthy choices

Take care of your body and mind during times of loss and grief. Your body needs all the help you can give it. It is normal for healthy habits and routines to lose priority during the initial stages of grief. Returning to our healthy habits and routines can serve as an anchor that holds us in the present and provides a sense of normal. Loss and grief can be very physically demanding and sometimes damaging. When possible make healthy choices, and use this time of change to grow into new healthy habits.

Exercise

Human bodies are built to move and be active; this is well documented. When possible maintain any exercise routine practiced before your loss and grief. If you do not have a routine exercise program, with your doctor's approval, aim to exercise at least 30 minutes most days. The 30 minutes does not have to occur at one time. You can break it into smaller increments and still receive benefit. For example, try a 15-minute walk at lunch and again after work. Body movement helps the body feel energized. So, get up and move when energy levels are low even a little exercise can make a difference. To function at its maximum our body needs to move every hour.

As an added benefit, exercise actually causes the body to release hormones that will improve mood and reduce stress. Exercise can also be very meditative. Try walking meditation to benefit both the body and the mind.

Nutrition

What we take into our body makes a difference. Eat a healthy diet to support and fuel your body and mind. Drink enough water to keep your body well hydrated. If you are isolated during your grief, good nutrition may be more challenging. Eating alone can be difficult, so you may not be eating enough healthy, well-balanced meals to get adequate nutrition. If you are losing weight, this is probably why; and over time this will negatively impact your health. Find a way to eat right. Create rituals and meal time activities, eat slowly and mindfully, schedule time with family and friends around meal times. Do anything that gets you eating healthy!

Rest and Sleep

It is common to have difficulty sleeping when experiencing loss or grief. Especially during grief recovery your body needs your support. Appropriate sleep is one of the best gifts you can give your body.

Rest and sleep are critical to healing and maintaining a healthy body. Getting enough rest and sleep helps our brain and body function better. Sleep improves brain function and helps with reasoning, problem solving, and paying attention to detail. Sleep helps regulate our mood, energy, and ability to focus. Inadequate or excessive sleep increases our chances of developing depression. Sleep deprivation can trigger some of the same negative outcomes as grief. You can support your body by getting enough rest and sleep during this time.

If you are having difficulty with sleep, here are some easy steps you can take that typically help improve sleep. Establish a sleeping pattern by going to bed and getting up at the same time every day. Develop a bedtime ritual that prepares your mind and body for rest. Consider listening to nature sounds, music or meditation tapes when going to bed. An hour or two before bedtime try to avoid the use of electronic screens. Also avoid consuming large amounts of food, caffeine or alcohol. You may find the action exercise on sleep to be helpful; it is located in Chapter 3, number 31.

Breath

Proper breathing is one of the easiest ways to improve our physical and mental health. And best of all it is free! Yes, we have been breathing all our lives. Nevertheless, most of us could significantly improve our breathing skills. Oxygen is the only body nutrient that we must take in constantly or we die within minutes. We rarely think about our breath. Proper breathing can calm the body, slow the heart, lower blood pressure, and help control pain. Deep breathing can decrease inflammation, improve heart health, boost the immune system, and probably even increase longevity. I feel so strongly about the power of breath that Chapter 2 is fully dedicated to breathing practices.

Strengthen Mental Health

Mental health is impacted by grief. Review the coping skills you have learned from previous difficult life experiences. Over a lifetime we all develop skills in adapting to change and struggles. Consciously choose to use those skills as you deal with your grief. You are stronger than you think. Believe in your strength.

The brain is one of the most complex and least understood organs. Only in recent years have we developed the ability to scientifically study the brain. In ways not yet fully understood, biology, psychology, and social forces all come together to affect our mental health and how we relate to the world. Leading edge research has investigated and concluded that mindfulness and meditation change not only our outlook on life but the very structure of the neural network in our physical brains. Actual measurable structural changes occur in the brain tissue of meditation practitioners. It might be worth mentioning that mindfulness and meditation practitioners have been observing and studying the mind for over two thousand years, and the standard techniques used are a result of that study.

Suffice it to say, all of the brain related research, although interesting, is beyond the scope of this book. Here we are simply interested in moving toward grief recovery. However, some clarification of terminology may be helpful. When I use the term mind, I am referring to that part of the brain that seems to hold thought and feelings and consciousness. I use thoughts to identify the chatter our mind creates as it analyzes our past and prepares for the future.

Stress

Reduce the stressors in your life as much as possible. Grief is enough stress at one time. Significant documented evidence advises that stress increases vulnerability to health problems. Stress also impairs our problem-solving skills and decreases our ability to think clearly and creatively.

Most of us have a 'go to' stress response. It may be a healthy response like exercising or talking with friends. It may be an unhealthy response like over-eating, over-drinking, gambling, or participating in risky behaviors. Be aware that during grief a stress relieving activity can become maladaptive and cause more problems. Limiting or discontinuing the use of drugs and alcohol during high stress times is helpful, as over-use can create an entire new set of stressors.

Pay attention. Think. Take care of yourself. If you remain mindful, you know when you are getting yourself in trouble.

Anxiety

(thoughts are typically focused on the future)

It is normal to worry about the future when a significant loss occurs; anxiety is closely tied to worry about the future. One way to control anxiety is by planning and doing whatever prepares you for the future while remaining solidly grounded in the now. Use your resources. Most of us have friends and family who want to support us as we plan and make decisions. When possible, select those with the best planning skills and let them help.

When we stay grounded in the current moment, our anxiety diminishes even in the worst of times. Anxiety escalates when the mind creates stories and catastrophes in the future. When the mind starts creating horror stories in the future, focus on breathing deeply and slowly. Focusing on your breath helps to ground you in the current moment.

Depression

(thoughts are typically focused on the past)

Grief and depression symptoms are closely related. Therefore, it is difficult to know if grief also includes some clinical depression. There are specialists and others in your situation that are ready and willing to help. It might be helpful to attend a support group for grief recovery or try a specialist in grief recovery counseling prior to medication. This will help you and your doctor determine if an antidepressant medication might help. There is no reason to extend suffering when help is readily available.

Photo: Cheryl Muck

Recognize and stop unhelpful thoughts

Our minds are a little bit like children; they give us more of what gets our attention. If we give negative thoughts too much attention, our mind will continue to give us more negative thoughts. It is difficult to stop negative thoughts even when we know they are not helpful. Try focusing your attention on positive thoughts. This will help keep you from becoming trapped on the negative-thought treadmill.

An effective way to decrease erroneous or unhelpful thoughts is to gently recognize and acknowledge them. Smile at the mind's silliness. Consciously ignore unhelpful thoughts and replace them with more positive thoughts. You have a choice! You can believe all the crazy thoughts your mind generates to keep itself busy, or you can mindfully stop your mind when it makes stuff up!

Most minds have some ingrained thought trails (neuro networks) that are negative, erroneous or unhelpful. Learn to recognize them and take action to close those trails. If you pay close attention, you can gain control over your thoughts. Below are some common unhelpful thought trails and some ideas to help close those trails.

Negative Filtering

We typically focus more on negative than on positive experiences/events. This is a factor of genetic selection. We are more likely to survive if we can identify potentially negative injurious events. Become aware of your own negative filter. Learn to shift your negative filter to the positive by consciously identifying and focusing on positive things.

Example Negative Filtering Mind Chatter:

I hate driving in the city. This traffic is horrible! I know someone is going to cut me off any minute.

Just stop - relax and sing along with the radio.

I love the songs they have on right now!

Oh, dang it! That car is cutting me off! Am I invisible or something?

HONKING and GESTURING. Is she not paying attention or did she do it on purpose? Who does she think she is? Why is her time more important than mine! Why does this always happen to me?

How to Turn It Around:

- When you are feeling picked on or thinking bad things always happen to you, stop and take a logical look at reality. As in the above example, you drove 20 minutes in traffic surrounded by hundreds, maybe thousands of cars. During that 20 minutes, you were cut off or put in danger by two drivers. Remind yourself there were many more attentive and considerate drivers than there were bad.

- Instead of seeing other drivers as competitors think of them as team members on the road together. We are all on our way to do important stuff! Notice the helpers and strive to be one.

- Now think about those two drivers. Allow your mind to think about what horrible things may have happened in their day! Once you have visualized those bad life situations, allow compassion to enter your heart. Smile and mentally send them love and hope and better times.

- Yes, watch out for the bad drivers to assure your safety but spend more time thinking and appreciating the drivers that are going about their day just like you! Some are just routinely going to work, home, school, to meet friends, or to shop. Some are picking up a sick child, going to a funeral, returning home after receiving a terminal diagnosis, going to check out a nursing home for mom, or some other crisis. You get the idea.

- Think more about the considerate and attentive drivers. Simply send love and compassion to all the aggressive or thoughtless drivers. The traffic won't change, but your life will improve as you focus on the positive instead of the negative encounters.

Personalizing

Our minds tend to automatically blame ourselves when something negative happens. There is value in evaluating our part when something goes wrong. However, much of the time whatever happens has little or nothing to do with us. Even though we can only see the world through our perspective, we it work diligently to make connections. If no connections exist, our mind may create stories to make sense of what has happened.

Example Personalizing Mind Chatter:

Oh, there's Sally! I need to finish my errands but I would love to sit and have a tea with her. I'll wave her down. It will be so nice to have a little break and someone to talk to.

Did she see me? I'll try again. She should have seen me that time! Oh my, what have I done to piss her off?

Did I remember to send her the thank you note for the flowers? I thought I did.

I shouldn't have cried on her shoulder! Maybe she didn't feel comfortable being around me or didn't know what to say. Now she doesn't want to be friends!

It is all my fault ... I'm sad and not as much fun as I used to be.

Oh wait ... she is coming over to say hi!

How to Turn It Around:

- Teach yourself to recognize when your mind is making up stories and gently stop those thoughts.
- Learn to believe only those thoughts you know for sure to be true.
- Remember the behavior of others is rarely about us. Other people's behavior is usually about them.

Catastrophizing

We all know people who awfulize and catastrophize everything beyond reality. We all have this tendency to some extent. Human minds are genetically selected towards foreseeing disaster to save us from physical harm. While this may have worked well for cave dwellers, it does not work so well in the twenty-first century.

Example Catastrophizing Mind Chatter:

My knee keeps having that strange twinge in it when I go down a step. Just ignore, it will go away. No, my knee is injured, I've hurt it. I think it is bad.

Maybe I need to see the doctor. I don't have time to go to the doctor. I don't want to spend the money to go to the doctor. If I go to the doctor, he is going to do a bunch or tests; and then they will find something bad - I know something is wrong.

Then I will have to have surgery to fix it and I don't have the time or money to have surgery!

But if I don't have surgery, I will end up in a wheelchair for the rest of my life. I don't have anyone to take care of me if I end up in a wheelchair!

OMG my life is over!

How to Turn It Around:

- Though amusing when you read it, our minds tend to run away periodically. We know it is a grand leap from knee pain to the wheelchair. But our minds create those thoughts, and then we listen to the silliness. Make the effort to pay attention to your thoughts and pull them back to reality!

- Train the mind to observe reality more accurately and to stop creating catastrophizing thoughts.

- Mindfulness and meditation are extremely helpful tools for training the mind. When we train our minds to stay focused on the now or at most the next thirty minutes, we can handle almost anything. It is the unknown future that we find difficult to handle.

Polarizing and Generalizing

Generalizing is our tendency to see the entire world or a single event in the same way. When we polarize we take a single life event to one end of the continuum or the other and then generalize it to our entire life. This is rarely, if ever, an accurate perception.

We relate to the extremes when our mind is being lazy. It requires mental effort and skill to tease out the truth which is almost always somewhere in the middle.

Example Polarizing and Generalizing Mind Chatter:

I am all alone. Everyone leaves me. I can't rely on anyone to be here when I need them!

My father left when I was 10. My boyfriend dumped me when I was 16. My friend left me and went to another school when we graduated. My parents died.

I am all alone. No one really loves me. I will always be alone. I will die alone.

How to Turn It Around:

Find some balance. Sometimes we have strong feelings left over from past hurtful events. Therefore, we connect with either one end of the continuum or the other instead of the middle.

- When caught in the extremes, remind yourself that the middle way is a better path.

- Focus on your breath to relax your body until you feel more relaxed.

- Take a moment to logically evaluate your thoughts and think of life examples that don't fit your current extreme point of view. This will help lessen the tendency to generalize.

- Moderate those extreme thoughts and come to balance. Decrease the tendency to polarize by letting go of thoughts stuck in an extreme end of a continuum.

Use positive affirmations

Positive affirmations are a very effective and simple way to transition from negative to positive thought patterns. The problem with negative thoughts is that they turn into self-prophecies. When we have negative thoughts about ourselves, those thoughts drag us down, and we become less than our best selves. Negative thoughts are self-sabotaging and create negative patterns that repeat in our lives.

Many ancient teachings extol the power of thoughts to create our life. The Bible states, "As we think, so we become." The Dhammapada says it this way "All that we are is the result of what we have thought; it is founded on our thoughts, it is made up of our thoughts." One of my favorite quotes also speaks to this truth:

Watch your thoughts
For thoughts become words
Watch your words
For words become actions
Watch your actions
For actions become habits
Watch your habits
For habits become character
Watch your character
For character becomes your destiny.

Author unclear - widely attributed to Frank Outlaw,
Lao Tzu, Ralph Waldo Emerson, the Buddha, etc.

Using daily positive affirmations can change your life for the better. They can keep your mind upbeat and positive. Those who consistently use positive affirmations report a happier and more positive life. And the best news - it is free, relatively quick and painless.

Human minds are genetically wired to capture and remember negative experiences and outcomes. Which memory is more important for survival — remembering where there is a grove of wild apples or remembering which cave houses the tiger den? The negative memory tied to the tiger den always wins! So, when our minds are not busy, our thoughts and ruminations trend to the negative. In today's world, some of our stress and unhappiness is a result of our genetic wiring toward remembering negative events tied to danger and fear.

Positive affirmations can help override this selective genetic wiring. Properly applied, positive affirmations help improve our performance, our state of mind, and even our health. If we have happy thoughts, we produce chemicals that make us feel happy. Negative, fearful, or angry thoughts produce chemicals that reinforce fear and anger. Research shows that thoughts and their related chemicals actually change the brain on a cellular level. Neurons in the brain connect and attach thoughts and memories. If we connect specific thoughts with specific feelings or memories, they soon become neurologically connected. Brain cells that fire together become wired together. For example, when children perform poorly on a test they might get into trouble at home. Soon taking tests become connected to fear which produces more bad outcomes resulting in poor test taking skills. Positive affirmations work by interrupting and ultimately re-wiring positive connections over negative neuro connections.

Basically, we can change and sculpt our brain in the same way that we work out to sculpt our muscles. Our thoughts produce emotions and feelings. Our feelings and emotions trigger production of brain chemicals that create physical responses like stress, fear, relaxation, happiness, or whatever. Positive affirmations, prayer, meditation, mindfulness all allow us to take control of our thoughts and ultimately change our lives. With time, we can re-wire our own brains. Positive mental exercises create positive mental patterns and then, over time, we begin to think and act differently which further changes our lives. If you want to learn more about how your brain changes, research "neuroplasticity."

Getting started with positive affirmations

1. There are no right or wrong techniques for working positive

affirmations into your daily life. Try several and figure out what works best for you. Here are some examples: Use positive affirmations as passwords. Place post-it notes with positive affirmations in frequently used locations. Create a set of index cards with positive affirmations and review them daily. Set a repeating calendar event with an affirmation as the content. Use your phone to create a recording of your favorite affirmations and listen to them when walking, exercising, or at bedtime. Set a phone alarm with the affirmation as the content.

2. To be most effective, positive affirmations must be read or stated at least daily. In the beginning, you may want to do them more than once a day. Consistently reading or saying the affirmation(s) is the most critical element for success. Although it is fine to talk about your affirmations with friends or family, they are only meant to impact your own subconscious mind.
3. Affirmations are most effective on the subconscious mind, where they gradually become part of who you are. You cannot think the statements into reality. There is no need to dwell on or think about each affirmation at length; just read or say each one daily, and thereby place it in the subconscious to do its work. Over time they become real as your subconscious mind hears and accepts them as reality. When we begin to simply act as if the affirmation is true, our very actions make them true.
4. Many affirmations start with "I am." Here is an example: "I am filled with joy." However, it could easily be written in other ways such as, "Joy fills my life." The idea is to create a positive statement about yourself which overrides an existing negative mental belief you want to change. Writing your own is probably most effective. However, the internet is full of sample positive affirmations. You can select ones that help you grow or write your own as you become more familiar with them.
5. Research shows that stating the positive affirmation in the present tense strengthens its influence. For example: "I am grateful" is stronger than "I will be more grateful" which places gratitude always in the future. Write the affirmation as if the feeling, self-belief, or statement is already true and present in your life.

6. Make your affirmations credible and achievable. They are most effective when they are realistic and relevant to your life. Affirmations should be a stretch but believable and achievable. Once you arrive at an affirmation, you can always revise it for a further stretch.

Photo: Cheryl Muck

Establish constructive habits

In psychological terms a habit is defined as an action that is automatically triggered in response to a specific contextual clue. That sounds more complicated than it is. For example, you automatically put on your seat belt (action) after getting in the car (contextual cue). It is not something you think about, consider, or consciously decide to do. Much of our behavior is habitual or triggered by a place or event. Initially all behaviors are mindful and intentional. Even mindful behaviors may gradually become routine habits void of mindfulness.

Research shows that any behavior repeated in response to an event (contextual cue) becomes an automatic behavior or habit after an average of 66 days. This time line shortens or lengthens dependent upon the individual and how complex the task. If you want to change a behavior or establish a habit, set a target of at least 9 to 12 weeks knowing that the behavior will get progressively easier as time passes, and it becomes a habit. After the habit is well established, an occasional break in routine does not weaken the habit. However, a sustained break in routine may require another habit establishment period.

Write it down! Research shows that a written goal is more likely to occur. Post your habit goal where you see it every day to further strengthen the habit. You may also want to develop a 90-day log and place a star on the log (or calendar) each day that you accomplish the goal. Research shows that getting a reward, even a small one, reinforces a new habit. Review your actions weekly and watch your progress; note how it gets easier over time.

Example goal: I am taking actions to live a more grateful life.

> Example plan: After brushing my teeth in the morning I look in the mirror, smile, and remind myself of at least 3 things for which I am currently grateful. I have placed a sticky note on my mirror to remind me to do this! I am adding a smiley face to the note every morning I meet the goal.

Here are simple steps to create a new habit:

1. Decide on a goal that you want to achieve to improve your life.
2. Choose a simple daily action to move you towards your goal. Keep it simple and doable. Once that goal is met, you can decide to advance to a more challenging action.
3. Plan when and where you will take the action. For best results, be consistent. It is best to choose an event you do daily.
4. Write down, plan, and post your goal. Create a visual flag or

reminder cue if that is helpful.

5. Every time you encounter that time and place or event, do the action. Once your action is completed, check it off on a tracking record.
6. Remember to give yourself positive feedback as you work toward creating your new habit. This can be a simple, *Yes! I am proud of myself!* or the stars on your log.
7. It gets easier with time. Typically, within 66 days you will find you are doing the action automatically without conscious decision or debate. If it takes you a little longer, don't give up! Consciously and mindfully continue taking the desired actions until it becomes automatic.
8. Reward yourself when you turn your goal into a habit. Congratulations, you created a positive habit to improve your life!

Photo: Cheryl Muck

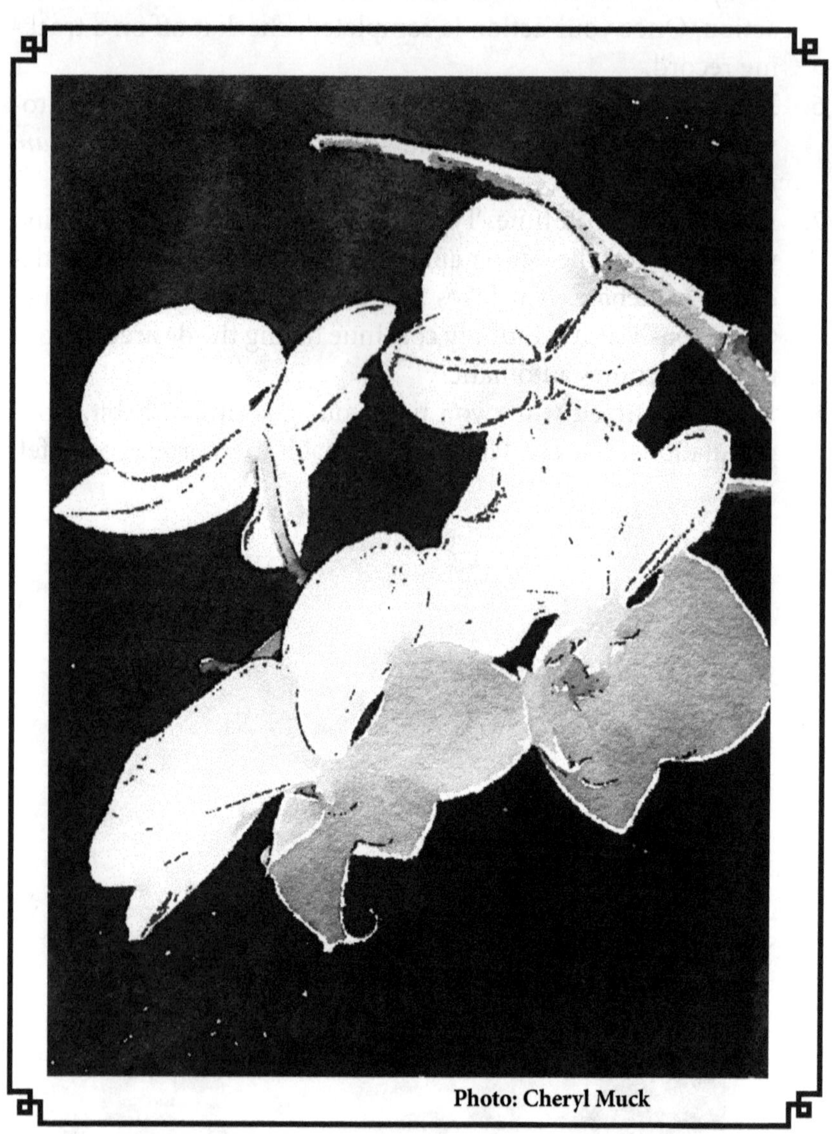

Photo: Cheryl Muck

CHAPTER 2 BREATHING PRACTICES:

Take a breathing break to calm the body

Breathing best supports our health and wellness when it comes from the abdomen. Keep the chest, shoulders and neck relaxed; they should not be involved in breathing. Expand the belly, sides and lower back all at the same time which draws breath fully into the lungs allowing the diaphragm to flatten and the ribs to flare out. Breathe in through the nose and fully exhale through the nose or mouth. The exhale should be slightly longer than the inhale. Research at the Robert Wood Johnson Medical School at Rutgers University found that on average most people reach a proper balance when breathing in 11 second cycles, with the out breath slightly longer than the in breath.

Average American breath rates range from 12 to 18 breaths per minute, faster than ideal. When we consciously slow our breath, we trigger vagus nerve activity, which slows our heart rate and digestion and decreases our inflammatory response. The body's relaxation response, the parasympathetic nervous system, is automatically initiated when we deepen and lower our breath rate to about 5 to 7 breaths per minute. Learning to periodically breathe deep and slow will support relaxation and wellness during your grief recovery.

Learning to control your breath may be the easiest way to improve your mental and physical health. In addition, routine breath practice also serves as an anchor for concentration and awareness of the moment. Some people find certain breathing exercises more helpful than others, so experiment and find which work best for you. There are many breathing practices; most are similar but each have their own unique focus.

This chapter provides helpful tips and concrete examples to get you started on a mindful breathing practice. Chapter 3 asks you to “Take a Breathing Break” before and after each action exercise. These breathing practices may benefit you more than any other suggestion found in this book. Please try it, even if it seems too simple to help. Remember the magic is in the doing rather than the thinking.

The remainder of this chapter provides you with specific examples to help you establish a healing breath practice. Breathing practice tips:

- The following pages outline simple and effective breathing practices. Many more can be found through an internet search.

- When you first start a breathing practice, you may find it helpful to set your phone alarm or a timer for 3-5 minutes of mindful breathing. Over time you may decide to gradually increase or decrease the time based on what you find most useful. After practicing for a period of time, you will learn to sense when your body has relaxed and benefited from the exercise.

- In the beginning a verbal guide can be helpful, but it will not be long before you can do the breathing practice on your own any time or any place.

- You may decide to record the breath practices on your phone for your personal use.

- I recorded these breath practices, and they are freely available for your use any time. Simply go to my YouTube channel.

Basic mindful breathing

This is a basic breathing practice. There is no need to control or do anything special as you breathe. Simply breathe with awareness, and your body will automatically begin to relax.

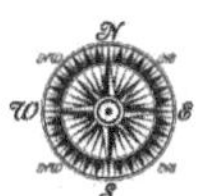

Breathe normally without changing the rhythm of the breath. Simply NOTICE your breathing. Breathe in through the nose and notice the pause. Breathe out through the mouth (blow a slow steady stream out pursed lips)and notice the pause.

Think only of the breathing; stay present with the feeling of the breath in the body. Notice where you most feel your breath — it may be in your chest, your abdomen, around your nostrils, or elsewhere.

Stay present with the breath.
Continue focusing on the breath.

When you realize your mind has wandered, gently come back to your breath without judgement or shame. Breathe in through the nose, pause; breathe out through the mouth (blow a slow steady stream out pursed lips), pause. Notice and follow your breath. Think only of the breathing. Stay present with the feeling of the breath in the body.

Repeat until you feel totally relaxed or for the time you have allotted.

Conscious Breathing Practice

This technique helps quiet a busy or ruminating mind.

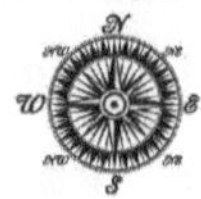

Sit quietly and comfortably. Begin observing and thinking about your breath. Follow the breath sensations. Focus on being aware of your breath.

I am breathing in
I am breathing out

I am breathing in
I am breathing out

Breathing in
Breathing out

Breathing in
Breathing out

In
Out

In
Out

Photo: Michael Smith

Be present with each breath. When body sensations or thoughts arise, simply identify them and allow them to pass like clouds in the sky. Without judgement, gently return focus to your breath. Start anew and just follow the breath sensations. Don't try to change anything; just focus on being aware of your breath.

The Mona Lisa Smile Breathing Practice

Typically, this breathing practice is good for mood elevation and increasing the level of happiness. Anytime we engage the smiling muscles, the brain and body respond as if we are happy. Our body does not know the difference between a "fake" or real smile! When smile muscles are engaged, our body releases mood elevating chemicals which then support ongoing happiness.

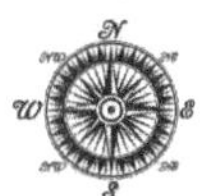

Smile softly - slowly breath in - slowly breath out
Smile softly - slowly breath in - slowly breath out
Continue until you begin to relax

Follow your normal breath rhythm
Stay softly aware of your Mona Lisa smile
Stay softly aware of your breath in and your breath out

When you lose focus on your breath, simply notice without judgement. Smile at your mind. Thank it for thinking and worrying and problem solving for you all day long. Smile and tell your mind you don't need its help right now. Smile and tell your mind that everything is fine; it can relax. Smile again and gently return to your breathing.

Smile softly - slowly breath in - slowly breath out
Smile softly - slowly breath in - slowly breath out
Continue until you relax

Once relaxed, follow your normal breath rhythm
Stay softly aware of your Mona Lisa smile
Stay softly aware of your breath in and your breath out

Counted Breathing Practice

Many people find this helpful when feeling drowsy or distracted since counting increases mental focus.

Sit quietly and focus on your breathing
Do not change it - just be with your breath
Identify any tense muscles
Focus on any tense muscles until they relax
Relax any tension in your body
Once you feel relaxed begin counting your breath:

Breathing in 1, breathing out, 1
Breathing in 2, breathing out, 2
Breathing in 3, breathing out, 3
Breathing in 4, breathing out, 4
Breathing in 5, breathing out, 5
Breathing in 6, breathing out, 6
Breathing in 7, breathing out, 7
Breathing in 8, breathing out, 8
Breathing in 9, breathing out, 9
Breathing in 10, breathing out, 10

Return to 1 and continue the cycle until you finish your breathing practice.

When you lose focus on your breath, simply label any distraction (itching, thinking, pain, listening, etc.). Then, gently place the labeled distraction on a leaf floating down the stream of your mind. Watch it gently float away.

Once released, gently return to your breathing practice without judgement.

Sit quietly and focus on your breathing
Do not change it - just be with your breath
Relax any tension in your body

Breathing in 1, breathing out, 1
Breathing in 2, breathing out, 2
Breathing in 3, breathing out, 3
Breathing in 4, breathing out, 4
Breathing in 5, breathing out, 5
Breathing in 6, breathing out, 6
Breathing in 7, breathing out, 7
Breathing in 8, breathing out, 8
Breathing in 9, breathing out, 9
Breathing in 10, breathing out, 10

Return to 1 and continue the cycle until you finish your breathing practice.

Relaxation Breathing Practices

Slow deep breathing triggers the body's relaxation response. This breathing can lower stress and also helps when unable to sleep. When new to the practice, deep slow breathing may cause hyperventilation, so if you become dizzy simply return to your normal breathing pattern.

Deep Breathing Practice with Counting

Sit or lie quietly.

Breathing in ... counting 1, 2, 3, 4
Pause ... counting 1, 2, 3, 4

Breathing out ... counting 1, 2, 3, 4, 5, 6
Pause ... counting 1, 2, 3, 4, 5, 6
(notice and maintain the slightly longer exhale)

If a thought or anxiety arises, acknowledge its presence without judgement and simply return to the slow deep breathing and counting. Repeat this practice for five minutes or until you feel totally relaxed. Sit or lie quietly.

Breathing in ... counting 1, 2, 3, 4
Pause ... counting 1, 2, 3, 4

Breathing out ... counting 1, 2, 3, 4, 5, 6
Pause ... counting 1, 2, 3, 4, 5, 6

Deep Breathing Practice without Counting

Breathe in deeply through the nose - remain aware of the physical sensations created,
Pause.
Breathe out through the mouth - blow slowly out pursed lips, aware of sensations.
Pause.

If a thought or anxiety arises, acknowledge its presence without judgement and simply return to the slow deep breathing. Focus on the sensation of breathing in through the nose and out through the lips. Repeat this practice until you feel totally relaxed or for your allotted practice time.

Photo: Cheryl Muck

Breathing and Visualizing Light Practice

Visualization is a powerful mental exercise. Use this breathing practice to acknowledge and transform any strong emotion you wish to move through. This example uses anger as the negative emotion. But you can replace it with any other negative emotion such as fear, stress, anxiety, guilt, grief, etc.

Take a few minutes to breathe and heal your anger.

Breathe in cleansing light.
Breathe out tension and anger.

Imagine you are breathing in white light.

See the pure white light burning through your anger.
Breathe out remembering the burning
Allow your anger to dissolve and crumble away into smoke and ashes.

Now imagine that light gradually becoming more violet with each in-breath.

See the violet light washing through your mind and spirit purifying every cell.
With each out-breath release all the tension and anger in your body.

Now imagine that light gradually turning green with each in-breath.

Feel the green light healing your body, mind and spirit.
With each out-breath rejoice in your freedom from anger.

Photo: Cheryl Muck

Photo: Cheryl Muck

CHAPTER 3 DOING THE WORK:

46 Practices to Support Healing

This chapter reminds us that life requires practice. Practice in the sense that we are never done or complete. We are always growing and changing. Every moment is different from all others. While continual change brings us pain, it also creates much of the wonder and glory of life. Practice is about the decisions and actions we take. Practice is about doing and learning and growing. It is not about being finished or perfect or done. It is about striving forward. As that is true of life, it is also true of grief.

Grief is always related to change; it is the healing process humans experience as a result of loss. Change and grief are natural even as we long to escape them. Grief is ever present, waxing and waning from moment to moment.

There are conscious practices that can support your grief process. These practices will not stop your grief, but they will help you move forward through your grief. They are not complicated — anyone can benefit from them. Yes, even you can benefit from them! But there is a trick to it; you have to do them. To heal requires time, action and practice.

The practices in this chapter each have a reading, two breathing practices, an action exercise and a positive affirmation to carry into your life.

Each practice starts with a reading. You may find some of them speak to you more than others. Don't worry about that. Our response is related to our own life experiences. Just read and take in what you find most helpful. You will know which readings are of most value for you.

Positive self-care requires action as well as thoughts. Completing the provided action exercises may help you move gently forward day by day. The exercises can help you consciously move into a healthy future. If one doesn't resonate for you that is fine; simply take any action that helps you move positively into the future.

Each breathing practice is a resting place. They provide a few moments to rest and relax your body and mind as you "Take a Breathing Break". When you stop and mindfully breathe, it naturally calms your body. A tense body can sabotage healing. Mindful breathing helps cultivate a calm body.

Positive affirmations are suggested to help you move in the direction you want. To shift your thought patterns in a positive direction, try the affirmations or make up your own. Positive affirmations engage our subconscious minds in the present to influence our beliefs and behaviors in the future. In my experience, they work. Try them and decide for yourself.

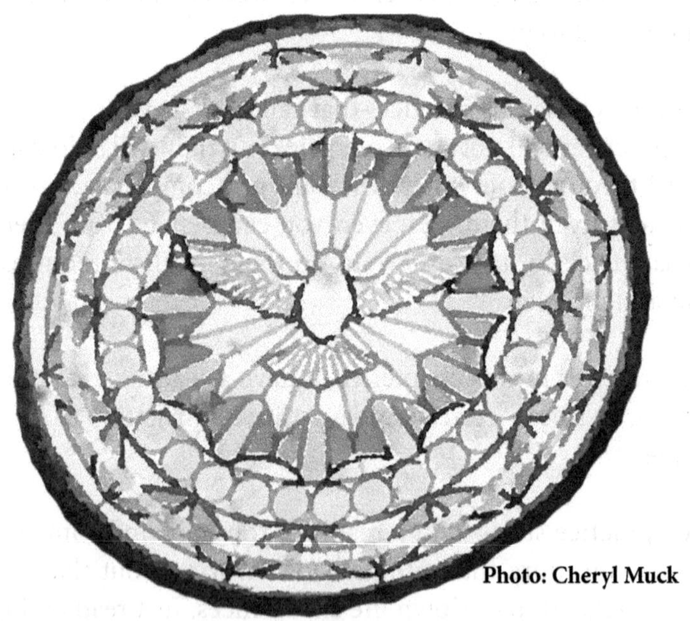

Photo: Cheryl Muck

Do What Works Best for You

My personal and professional experience with hospice care have taught me that the way through grief is to be present with the loss. We may never get over the loss of a loved one, but we can lovingly acknowledge our grief with compassion and go on with a full life. This chapter offers specific resources that may help you on your grief journey.

You may want to create a habit of mindful self-care using this book. If you complete a reading/exercise every day, it will help you establish a habit of self-care. You may want to read and practice one reading/exercise over and over until you feel finished with it, or you may complete them one at a time. You may choose to read them in order or randomly. If you are in the initial stages of grief, a reading or exercise may be too painful - simply pass it by and come back to it later.

I invite you to make notes and comments in this book to make it your own. If you decide to move around in the book, the notes will help you navigate. This is your book and your healing - own them both. Whether you do the work now or leave it to the future - either way your personal notes will support the process.

Since everyone has their own individual strengths and opportunities for growth, some thoughts will be more helpful for you than others. Some may not ring true for you. Some may seem too painful. Don't worry too much about any of that. Just be open and mindfully take in each reading and exercise. Without personal judgement simply evaluate how each idea fits in your life. Try switching off your inner critic. Now is not the time to judge yourself or others. Allow reality to be what it is—neither right nor wrong. Be present with and simply accept the reality of what is, right here and right now. When you allow yourself to be present with your grief, without judgement, you support healthy personal growth and healing.

Take Action Toward Healing

The following practice sessions can be used to gain insights and support your grieving process. As we move through grief, every day is a new day. How we feel and how we cope will fluctuate as we progress through the process. Healing is happening right now as you strive to find your way. There is no wrong way. There is no right way. There is simply your way.

Use your own good judgement and do what works for you. You are the best judge of what is helpful. You are the only person who understands your grieving and healing process. Regardless of where you are on the grief path, each day strive to take some action which supports your healing progress.

Mindfully practicing self-love and compassion is the kindest thing you can do for yourself. You have suffered a great loss. It is good to take care of yourself as you would a friend. When we identify and acknowledge emotions as they arise, without judgement, we create an emotional maturity that gives life integrity and meaning. Ultimately, life is enriched when we practice emotional awareness and agility.

Photo: Michael Smith

Practice Session #1: Loss

Reading and contemplation

Change is the very foundation of life. Loss is our emotional response to change. No one gets through life without loss and grief. Grief is the healing process which helps us process our loss and re-engage with life. Little griefs may last minutes; big griefs may last years. Short or long, mindfulness supports recovery and a healthy transition to the other side of the grief process.

Some losses are evident to the world — the death of a loved one, separation/divorce, loss of job, robbery/rape/violent crime, loss of home or money. Some losses are typically viewed as good by society — loss of a goal (success), loss of job (retirement), loss of a dream (meeting a goal), etc. Grieving for losses that are not obvious or viewed as good by society can be particularly difficult.

Some losses are inevitable, and we can prepare for them. Our grief process and recovery is typically shorter when we prepare for and talk about the anticipated changes/losses. This requires a great deal of mindfulness (being present in the moment). When we are mindful of reality and the natural rhythms of life, we are better able to identify and be present with inevitable losses.

With expected deaths, mindfulness supports dealing with the loss. When we take time to talk honestly about upcoming loss and grief everyone benefits. It is helpful to allow all loved ones to voice their opinions and be involved in care decisions. We can support each other by mindfully listening and accepting other opinions without judgement. This allows everyone's thoughts and desires to be heard and considered in decisions. Whenever possible, thoughtfully make decisions based on the wishes and desires of the person(s) most closely impacted.

Take a breathing break

Action exercise:

Our minds and feelings and bodies are designed to experience loss, healing and recovery. Our very first actions in this world are about adapting to change. The baby is born, gasps for breath and cries. Our first big change has occurred. The safety and security of the womb is lost. Every change is a loss to be experienced, healed and recovered.

No one escapes loss and grief. You and everyone you meet is recovering from loss and experiencing grief. It is the nature of life.

Healing is happening, right here and right now. Be present and allow it to occur. Spend a few minutes contemplating how to heal from your pain and loss. Look into the future and visualize a day when you feel happy and whole. See yourself surrounded by people that love you. Breathe in that feeling of love and safety.

Take a breathing break

Return to life with a positive affirmation

My body, mind and soul are designed to heal

Practice Session #2: Mindful Grief

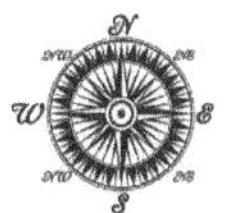

Reading and contemplation:

Grief is a process that takes time as it comes and goes and changes every day. When grief becomes intense, be mindful and accept what is happening. Consciously focus on your breathing and then gently let the wave of grief go as the intensity fades. Some losses stay with us forever, and we may never fully recover. But we can come out the other side changed and stronger. We can accept reality as it unfolds in each moment. We can be present and learn to live with the loss. We can stay grounded on our path forward each day.

When someone dies or departs from our life, we mourn. This response is normal, healthy and fully human. Staying present with our feelings moment by moment keeps us from projecting our current feelings into the forever of the future. Thus, mindfulness helps heal our brokenness one moment at a time. We can learn to accept the impermanence of all things, life, and relationships. Over time, we come to understand that even emotional pain is impermanent.

Mindfulness keeps us grounded in the here and now of this moment. If we live in the past or the future we are caught outside of reality. If our mind is focused on the past, we live in a time that no longer exists. If our mind lives in the future, we are in a time that does not yet exist. In reality, life can only be lived in this moment —here and now. The pain, the sadness, the difficulty can only be resolved or improved in the present moment, here and now.

Use mindfulness to keep anchored in reality, as it is, without judgement. As we better understand loss and grief, we learn to compassionately support ourselves and others without judgements of right or wrong. If we embrace our suffering with loving-kindness, we gradually find peace and a greater understanding of reality. We may even accept that someday we will experience joy and happiness again. The nature of life is change. Nothing, even the pain of sorrow, lasts forever.

Take a breathing break

Action exercise:

Sit quietly and really LOOK.

- Example: The chair. The plant drooping with the need for water. The sun shining across the room. Dust from the universe floating in the air. The deep reds of the rug. A shadow in the corner.
- Make no judgements or evaluations, just observe all that is here, in this space. Notice all the details that are normally ignored as background.
- Now your turn, look and really see, as if for the first time.

Sit quietly and focus on the sense of hearing. Truly HEAR. (Close your eyes if it helps.)

- Example: The bird singing out in the yard. The refrigerator running. Someone brushing their teeth down the hall. Rain gently dripping on the roof, flowing down the gutter and away. Car driving by. Airplane.
- Life going on all around. All worthy of attention, both the minuscule and the large.
- Now your turn. listen and really hear.

Sit quietly and focus on the sense of SMELL.

- Example: Left over breakfast. Dampness from the rain. Essential oil. Lingering coffee.
- Smell is an almost unnoticed experience. We have very few words to describe smells. Since smells are almost always associated with something, it is the sense that is most closely linked to memory. Dad's aftershave. Mom's doughnuts. Grandpa's black jack licorice gum. Friend's essential oil.
- Now your turn and really smell with your whole being.

Sit quietly. Be fully present and alive in this moment. Here. Now. No past; no future. Smile gently ... enjoy the peace of right now, right here. Nowhere to go. Nothing to do. Just resting in this glorious space ... aware of all that is here. No labels, no judgements, no comparisons. Just here, just now. Resting in the present moment, perfect even in all its imperfections. Ah ... this is mindfulness. Take this awareness into your day.

Sometime today do this same exercise with the senses of TOUCH and TASTE. Today allow your senses to keep you rooted in the current moment.

Take a breathing break

Return to life with a positive affirmation

I live a mindful life

Practice Session #3: Lifecycle

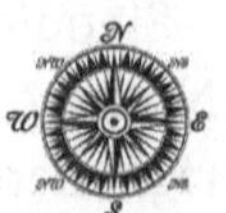

Reading and contemplation:

There is a natural order to all of life. The sun rises, shines, and sets. Summer follows spring and spring follows winter. The rhythms of life feel natural and right. We experience life as a cycle. Lifecycles frame the reality of our experience from the moment we are born to the moment we die.

My father was not a religious man, but he was one of the most spiritual people I have known, even if he would have never used that word. After years of illness, one day in his special way he told me he was ready to go. Here is the story he told me:

"I feel like a dry wheat field when it is ready for harvest. My body is brittle and stiff and easy to break; it hardly feels like my own any more. I remember when I was a young sprout, I was flexible and bent easily with no thought of breaking. And then I grew up strong and firm, blowing in the wind, soaking up the rain and the sun. Life was beautiful and full and good. But now I'm used up and dry, and those days are gone. It is time for the younger generation to have this field. I have had a good run. It was a wonderful life. Make sure you enjoy each stage of your life; they are all good in their own way."

May we all learn to accept the cycles of life with such grace. Thank you, daddy!

Just so you know, that memory still makes my heart ache after all these years. I want to see and hug and talk to him again. In some moments, the pain of his loss is not any less. But at this point in the grief cycle, I can acknowledge the pain and let it flow past like a cloud in the sky. I know the intensity will fade and the joy of remembering still makes my heart sing. I allow myself to feel the pain so that I can also feel the joy of memories and abiding love.

Every cycle of life has both joy and pain. Joy follows sorrow, as sunrise follows the darkness of night. Feelings come and go. Personally, I would not give up grief. To give up grief would require me to give up love, for grief is born of love. Life would be less without these cycles.

Take a breathing break

Action exercise:

Sit quietly, resting in this moment without judgement.

Take a few moments to think about something in your past that was difficult and you thought would never end.

Now spend a few moments considering how that dark cycle of time helped define who you are today.

What did you learn?
Have you grown?
Did that hard time help define who you are?

Take a few minutes to feel compassion for yourself as you live through this difficult time.

Each cycle of your life arises and will pass away.

Know that this too will pass.

Take a breathing break

Return to life with a positive affirmation

I appreciate each cycle of life.

Photo: Cheryl Muck

Practice Session #4: Change

Reading and contemplation:

The nature of life is change. Life is a process. We are meant to change and grow and progress. Relationships change and grow or end. Relationships with parents, children, friends, work colleagues, etc. are always in a state of change. Sometimes we expect relationships to stay the same or go on forever. This is not the way the world works, even if the mind wants it to be so.

When loss occurs, it feels like everything stops. But life aches to go on. Life cannot stand still — the world turns, work continues, the game goes on, the grass grows, dinner has to be served. There is nothing unfaithful about changing and growing and moving on. Anything alive is in a constant state of change.

When we suffer a loss, we sometimes become preoccupied with a specific perfect time and place. We idealize our lost love and our lost relationship. Love becomes better in memory than it was in reality. This is a normal process that helps us remember all the good. But at some point, it is helpful to recall that life is never perfect; relationships are never perfect.

When we learn to accept reality as it was and as it is, moving forward becomes simpler. We accept that our relationship was like all others both good and bad, however we define that. We remember that our loved one was not perfect. Perfect or not, our hearts still loved, and we were loved in return. In the balance, we are better because of love. We know we will never love another in quite the same special way. We accept other loves into our present life. We understand that although our loved one is physically gone, we will have a relationship with them for the rest of our lives. At the most unexpected times, a loved one will pop into our mind and inform the way we see an event, impact our decisions or actions, or fill our heart to overflowing with love and memories.

Take a breathing break

Action exercise:

Seasons cycle through the year. Storms develop, surround us and pass by. Pains come and go. Emotions arise and fade away. People enter and leave our lives.

"Nothing is permanent" is a simple and accurate statement that we all know to be true, and yet far from simple to accept. Change will always win no matter how hard we fight against it. It makes sense to surrender to change. Amazingly, life becomes more blessed and important and meaningful when we accept the certainty of impermanence.

Today, as you go through your day see every routine event through the eyes of impermanence. Hold each activity and encounter and person in the shining light of impermanence. Savor every moment, it will truly never come again. Each event is suddenly special. Each person is an encounter with the Holy. Drink in the amazing joy of being alive.

Take a breathing break

Return to life with a positive affirmation

**I accept change
as the natural flow of life**

Practice Session #5: Simplify

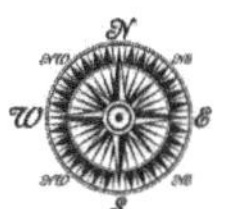

Reading and contemplation:

We live in a complex world. Our lives are rarely all we would like them to be. We make decisions and take actions that we regret, and then, we live as if we can't change it. Although it is probably not a good idea to make too many big changes after a major loss, it can be an opportunity to take inventory of your life.

In normal times, we unconsciously forget that life is continually changing. During loss and grief, we are painfully aware that life is continually changing. We come face to face with the reality of change. Life is impermanent. If we are blessed, we learn to fully appreciate and live in each moment, as it is.

In the midst of loss and grief, there can be a cathartic cleansing and a fresh start. It can be a time of renewal if we strive for that to be so. Life has very few opportunities to start fresh. Remember leaving home for school or work, starting a new marriage, or leaving the security of a good job? All can be stressful and create fear. But each of those events also gives us the opportunity to reevaluate who we are, to envision who we want to be, and to make changes in our life. Major life losses allow us this same opportunity.

Simplifying our life is usually a good thing. Don't automatically fill up every moment. Savor this quiet time and the freedom of time alone. Let go of things and activities that no longer serve. Listen to the heart. It is very wise and knows what is needed to live a wonderful life. It is OK to let go. Lighten the load. Live fully in each moment. Leave the baggage behind.

Take a breathing break

Action exercise:

Relax. Sit quietly. Let the world fall away. Rest. Simply do nothing for as long as you are comfortable resting in peace.

From this place of simplicity, consider what complicates life. Think about the baggage you want to set down, and simply never pick up again. Take your time. Consciously evaluate how your desired changes will impact your life. Be with your loss. Gently simplify and move into your new life. You are in charge of your life. Make it your best life.

Keep it simple. Keep it meaningful. Keep it honest.

Take a breathing break

Return to life with a positive affirmation

I keep my life simple and peaceful

Photo: Michael Smith

Practice Session #6: Flow Like a River

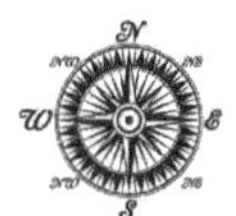

Reading and contemplation:

Like a river
some days feel peaceful and flow gently along.
Enjoy and rest in the peace.

> Then rapids arise and feelings tumble wildly about, out of control.
> Thoughtfully notice and stay aware of what creates the wild ride.

A river of emotions may become a flood and flow over it's banks or simply dry up.
Nourish yourself with positive thoughts and actions,
until the water returns to the natural stream.

> There may be boulders standing in the way of healing.
> Be like a river and allow yourself to flow around them.

No matter what we do, the river steadily flows to the ocean.
It is natural and instinctive. No effort required, just relax.
Let it happen without struggle.
The ocean refuses no river
each is worthy, accepted and welcomed home.

Like the river settles into the ocean
find peace out beyond the surging surf of life.
Relax into the whole, accepted and embraced.
Allow the ocean to wash you clean and heal your wounds.

Take a breathing break

Action exercise:

Today
Observe your emotions
Allow them to be as they are
Try not to get stuck in any emotion
Allow emotions to come and go and flow as they will

Today
Become an observer
Be present with your emotions
Experience each feeling as it arises
Watch each emotion gently flow into the past

Today
Emotions come natural
Emotions ebb and flow
Emotions move in and on through
All emotions are temporary and then depart

Take a breathing break

Return to life with a positive affirmation

I allow sorrow to flow through me without overcoming me

Photo: Cheryl Muck

Practice Session #7: Self-compassion

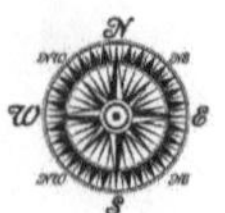

Reading and contemplation:

When we practice self-compassion, our view of the world changes, our hearts open, and our lives are transformed. Life becomes more loving, more meaningful, and more honest.

Self-compassion opens our hearts allowing us to see reality as it is, full of both joy and sorrow.

Having compassion first for ourselves ultimately supports our compassion for others. How do we give others compassion if we withhold it for ourselves? Self-compassion is never selfish. It is the first step to compassion for others.

For some reason, most of us find self-compassion difficult to master. As children in our culture, we observe and learn many self-pity behaviors but witness few examples of self-compassion. There is rarely anyone we treat as mean as we treat ourselves. The great religions teach compassion for others and for ourselves regardless of worthiness. Self-compassion is the cornerstone for building a life filled with love, connection, and oneness as we embrace ourselves and share our humanity with others.

Self-compassion helps us acknowledge and accept our problems as a normal part of being alive. We begin to see that life is not always within our control. We learn that our response to what happens is more important than what happens. We accept that life creates each of us, according to circumstances and that our specialness comes from our challenges. Our individual strengths, weaknesses and quirks are a result of the very challenges and losses we experience.

Self-compassion radically changes our lives. Yet, we are not taught it, and few of us learn it. What actions can you take to develop self-compassion?

- KINDNESS towards yourself is the first step on the path of self-compassion.
- EXPERIENCE your emotions; know they are transient and will be replaced.
- OPEN yourself to unconditional love and acceptance.
- LEARN to live without judgement of yourself or others.
- LOOK at life and see it honestly, without comparing, distorting, obsessing, or resisting.
- RELEASE the need for perfection. As the Zen saying goes, "You are perfect just as you are, and you could use a little improvement." Shunryu Suzuki
- KNOW that you are not alone; feel your connections with everyone and everything.

Take a breathing break

Action exercise:

Today, spend some time reflecting on self-compassion. Right now, think about each of the bullet items listed in the reading. Identify any specific behaviors or actions that you can take to develop those characteristics. Be as honest with yourself as you can be. If your performance is below what you want, determine how to work toward improving your self-compassion skills.

Today practice self-kindness as a starting point for nurturing self-compassion. Honestly think about what KINDNESS you can show yourself today and this week. Make a list and commit to do at least three acts of kindness for yourself this week. These could be things you already do for yourself, or they could be new kindnesses. Take a moment now to put those kindness activities on your calendar. If you have trouble accomplishing your acts of self-kindness, avoid judgement and negative self-talk, and simply reschedule it. Learn to treat yourself with compassion and you will probably become your own best friend in the process!

Take a breathing break

Return to life with a positive affirmation

Photo: Cheryl Muck

Practice Session #8: Self-pity

Reading and contemplation:

Self-pity happens to all of us from time to time. It is easy to become self-focused and self-absorbed, placing ourselves at the center of the universe. It is normal and simply human to have some of these feelings. Self-pity only becomes toxic when it turns into a habitual response to troubles.

Being stuck in self-pity takes many forms. We may believe our loss is not fair and wonder, "Why me?" Sometimes, we make comparisons and believe we got the short straw. Other times we may embrace our misery and even become comfortably attached to it. Occasionally, we may lose our identity to grief as it takes over our life. We may even crave the drama of being at the center of attention. Self-pity pulls us along many roads that we may not want to travel.

If we get stuck in self-pity, it is harder to grow and learn from our changing circumstances. The easiest way to step off the self-pity treadmill is to graciously offer self-compassion. Paradoxically, when there is self-compassion, there is no need or room for self-pity.

Take a breathing break

Action exercise:

Breathing in
I embrace myself
with compassion
Breathing out
I release
my losses

Breathing in
I embrace myself
with compassion
Breathing out
I release
my losses

Breathing in
Compassion
Breathing out
Loss

Breathing in
Compassion
Breathing out
Loss

Do this simple exercise several times in a row. Repeat until you feel more loving compassion toward yourself. Use this exercise routinely to foster more self-compassion. If it is helpful, you may even choose to set your phone alarm reminding yourself to repeat this exercise multiple times throughout the day. When the alarm buzzes, find a quiet space to be present, breath, and do the exercise. Then gently come back to the current moment. If you are with others, the restroom is a great retreat place to practice. If you are able, try walking outside while you do this exercise.

Take a breathing break

Return to life with a positive affirmation

I embrace self-compassion

Practice Session #9: Pity Party

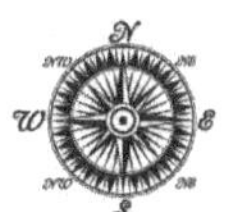

Reading and contemplation:

My mom was diagnosed with Parkinson's disease in her early 50s. Her dad had Parkinson's, so her disease had lots of fears and memories attached. It required daily management and was progressively degenerating, requiring routine trips to the specialist, changes in medications, and physical therapy. Mom did as well as any human could do in her situation; but it was not easy. On one visit to her neurologist, after years of treatment, he asked if she was feeling depressed. She told him she was feeling a little down and sorry for herself. Looking down he smiled and was quiet for a few minutes. Then, he looked up and told her she needed to have a good old pity party. She deserved it, she earned it, and by gosh she should have it. He told her to get down in that hole and really wallow in the unfairness of her medical problems. He told her to hold a worthy pity party and get it all out. Then close down the party, get over herself and move on. It could be a lot worse, and someday it might be. But not today. Today she should live her life fully and enjoy it. So, she did just that! She lived nearly thirty years with Parkinson's and she would occasionally share her Mona Lisa half smile and say, "Just having a little private pity party today. I'll be back to myself soon."

We can't stop loss. In each life, loss and the subsequent grief is an unavoidable reality. Sometimes, we feel it is just too much to take. One big loss, or an accumulation of many smaller losses may overcomes us. Occasionally, the best way to cope is to just sit down and host a pity party. There is nothing wrong with doing that once in a while! Just do it mindfully and be aware of maintaining balance.

Balance is key to working through grief. Hosting a personal pity party can help us be present with our pain. It is much better to be aware of and experience our pain than to ignore it. If ignored, the pain can fester and show up in other unhealthy ways. Get it out, let the light of exposure heal it.

Without balance, we may exaggerate our loss and move into a life of self-pity. A self-indulgent obsession on one's own life, circumstances, losses and disappointments leads to self-pity. We dwell on our losses and create stories in our head to keep the drama alive and current. This is very different from self-compassion. Self-compassion is a state of understanding and love and acceptance of loss. Self-compassion leads to a balanced resolution of the grief cycle, while self-pity promotes an ongoing state of pain and grief.

We create balance and walk the middle way when we embrace the reality of our loss and grief without amplifying it. Over time, as balance is reached, there is less need for a private pity party. Although we cannot avoid loss and grief, we can mindfully hold our experience of loss in a balanced awareness. This requires that we neither ignore nor exaggerate our pain, but rather walk the middle path.

Take a breathing break

Action exercise:

Host a PITY PARTY. It is always best to have a Private Pity Party. No sense in dragging anyone else into it. After all, it is your party, and who wants someone else there impacting the mood! I have experience with this; it has gotten me through many a bad time. Here are some tips on hosting a healthy Private Pity Party:

1. Establish a time frame. This is not healthy if it drags on too long. As we all know, every party has to end! Pull out your phone and set an alarm to tell you when to end the party. If you are not sure how long, start with 10 minutes. Although it doesn't seem like long, you will close with an equal amount of recovery time. A lot can happen in 20 minutes well spent.
2. This is a PERSONAL party, no one else allowed. Party in a safe and private place where no one else can hear. This party could get loud!

3. Immerse yourself in how difficult life is right now. No dwelling on the past or your future worries.
4. Focus on your current struggles. You can do this by talking to yourself, writing, crying, screaming, hitting pillows, whatever you want to do as long as it is not self-destructive. (Party no-no's: no physical injury, no alcohol, no drugs, nothing that will create harm. Those things negate the entire purpose of the party.)
5. Use no restraint. This is the time to get any pain, rage, resentment, and despair out of your mind and out in the open.
6. Once your Pity Party time alarm goes off, give yourself time to rest and recover, usually an equal time to the pity party. Set that alarm again.
7. Do whatever feels right for you — sleep, rest, listen to soothing music, meditate, contemplate the issues that came up without judgment or guilt. Think about all the positive people in your life. Take a walk alone or take a warm bath. You get the idea. Do what is right for you.
8. REPEAT as necessary. Do this often enough to support and allow your current experience of grief. Remember this is not a rehash of the past or a projection into the future. Stay focused on what is happening and going on right now.

Take a breathing break

Return to life with a positive affirmation

I am kind to myself

Practice Session #10: Using Positive Affirmations

Reading and contemplation:

2013 was one of those years that changed my life. My mother died that year. We were prepared; she had been ill such a long time. She was ready to move on. She made the choice to start hospice service, to stop going to the hospital, and finally to stop the medicines that were prolonging her life. I was lucky to have a wonderful mother. She loved me, and her unconditional love filled me with self-confidence. She taught me how to cook, sew, look out for myself, love unconditionally and most of all to always be kind.

Her death left a hole in my heart and life. I felt a bit adrift ... unmoored ... orphaned. I was relieved she no longer suffered. But it was hard to lose the first person I ever loved. It took longer to recover than I expected. I was not quite myself without her. For over 60 years I had worked to always be who she wanted me to be. Who was I without her vision of me?

I decided to try an old practice that had helped me in the past. The benefits of positive affirmations had seen me through another troubled time. So, I made a set of affirmations to help me heal and process through my grief. Using them once again helped me. You will find some of them in this book!

Many years ago, a life coach reminded me of what I had learned about positive affirmations in my nurse training years. She taught me how to create a daily positive affirmation practice. Although it seemed too easy to be helpful, I tried it. Within a month the practice created an amazing positive difference. Nine months later, I needed to make a new set of affirmations since most of them had already manifested in my life.

It is one of those things that words can't explain; it must be experienced to be understood. Talking or reading about it is useless. The magic is in the doing, commit to using a positive affirmation practice for at least 66 days and see for yourself!

Take a breathing break

Action exercise:

If you are ready to experience a positive affirmation practice, this process will help you get started. Get yourself a little spiral bound set of index cards in which to write your affirmations. The spiral index cards are readily available in the office supply section of many stores. Over the next few days or weeks create a set of positive affirmations that represent who you hope to be a year from now. Make up your own affirmations, select ones from this book, or go online and find some that represent who you want to be. Dream big; affirmations are powerful. You will surprise yourself! Keep adding to it until your personalized positive affirmation notepad is full. Start using your personalized affirmations today. There is no need to wait until you think they are perfect or done. Affirmations will naturally change and grow as you do!

Here is how I made my first set:

My life coach gave me a spiral bound set of multicolored index cards. My task was to fill the cards with positive affirmations that had meaning and purpose for me. Her instructions were to flip through and quickly read the cards daily. No need to spend time contemplating them! Simply set the affirmation in my subconscious. This made the process quick. It shouldn't take longer than a few minutes to simply flip through and silently read the entire set. I did that faithfully every day until the statements were mostly fulfilled and my first set of cards needed to be refreshed and renewed! It worked because I established a habit for the reading process. I found that reading them in bed last thing before sleep worked best for me.

In the beginning, it is very helpful to do your affirmations as a daily ritual and habit. Try not to have any expectations. Affirmations work on the subconscious level, so simply read them daily to place them in your subconscious. There is really no need to spend time thinking about them. Once I began meditating daily, positive affirmations became part of my routine life with less thought and ritual. I still pull out and review the entire set when I am feeling down or stressed. Remember positive affirmations impact our life by creating gradual subconscious movement toward "who we want to be."

Take a breathing break

Return to life with a positive affirmation

I grow and improve every day

Practice Session #11: Habits

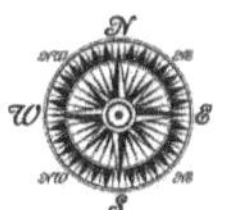

Reading and contemplation:

When we lose a loved one, we can become overwhelmed by the changes in our life. These life adjustments hit us over and over — every day, every week, every month, and every special occasion. If your daily life was closely tied to your loved one, you will have more adjustments. To a large degree this is related to the number of habits that direct our lives.

Our daily lives are typically filled with unconscious life directing habits. Most of us spend large portions of our life on "auto-pilot." We all establish routine habits for life efficiency, to free our conscious minds for other tasks. These "auto-pilot" functions are deeply ingrained. When we lose a loved one, our shared life habits become trigger points for memories. Here are some typical examples of habit triggers:

- I walk in the back door and head to the kitchen to give my spouse a kiss. I suddenly remember and stop. I am briefly back to the first anguish of loss.
- I get up on Saturday morning and automatically start preparing a leisurely weekend breakfast and grab two plates out of the cabinet. I sit down at the empty second placing and cry for my loss.
- I come home Friday from a late night at the office. I sit in the car and dread going into the house, concerned I will find someone drugged out in the den. Just then reality dawns on me. That will never happen again. I am overcome with the discord of unbearable grief and at the same time relief.

Our habitual responses and actions flood our life with memories - both good and bad. In the early phases of loss and grief, these memories can highjack our emotions and make us feel overwhelmed. It is tempting to try to deny and avoid those emotions. However, as we feel the painful jolts of change, we begin to heal when we stay present and experience our loss. This is the first step toward adapting and developing new habits and rituals. When we avoid our pain, we tether ourselves to an unconcluded past and our life may become limited in ways we can't even imagine. Experiencing and staying present with our loss can help us release our pain and create room for a fulfilling future.

Look at your rituals and habits. Mindfully consider how they serve you. Mindfully decide which habits or rituals you want to hold on to and which you want to lovingly and mindfully release. Make conscious decisions to release old habits that no longer serve you.

Take a breathing break

Action exercise:

Set your phone alarm for 10 minutes. Spend this time contemplating your lost relationship and what life habits were tied to that relationship. Which of your life habits were tied to your lost relationship? Were they Daily, Weekly, Monthly or Annually? Think about how the loss of those habits will impact you. Write them down if that is helpful.

Consider how you might develop new replacement habits while honoring disrupted habits. Are there new healthy habits you might want to develop to replace the habits which no longer serve you? Your life probably changed without your consent; however, you can have an active role in changing your future. Be mindful of how you think and behave today, as today's actions shape tomorrow. Consciously create new habits that move you in the life direction you wish to go.

Take a breathing break

Return to life with a positive affirmation

I foster positive habits

Photo: Cheryl Muck

Practice Session #12: We Are Connected

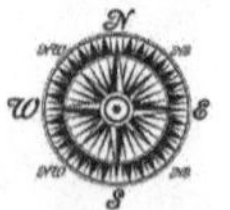

Reading and contemplation:

When we lose someone, we may feel lost and incomplete. Sometimes we feel as if a part of us is missing. This sense of separation assaults us because we exist in a physical world. In this reality, it is difficult to see that we are all connected. We can forget that we are never separate from someone we love. Our lives and those around us are interconnected and intertwined forever. The mystics and scientists agree that there is less separation than meets the eye.

When someone dies or departs from our life, we mourn their loss. We think they are gone forever, and yet, over time we see that they remain forever in our lives. Even in their going, they remain. They continue informing our decisions, our thoughts, our moods, and all that we are. When we truly love someone, they remain forever present in our heart and impact our lives as long as we live. Not only do they change our life, but as we impact others, they too impact others, and so each life forever ripples through all time. A single life creates endless ripples which continue from each moment to the next, from each life to the next. We are all one with another.

Here are some examples to think about:

Our bodies are continuations of our parents, grandparents, great grandparents going back to the beginning of time. Change any one of them, and we are changed. Each cell in our body has previously been other — water, soil, vegetables, the stars! At an atomic level, we are all continually shifting in and out of each other. Take a moment and experience this vast movement and communion with LIFE. Relax into the reality that we are always connected.

Photo: Cheryl Muck

the trees exhale
we inhale
we exhale
the trees inhale
the trees exhale
we inhale
we exhale
the trees inhale
the trees exhale
we inhale

If we are one with the breath of the trees, can we be less connected with our loved ones? We are forever connected. We are always complete, individual and yet also ONE together. Relax and feel the connection. We are never separate. Our wholeness is always present even when we feel incomplete or separate or lost.

Take A breathing break

Action exercise:

Sit comfortably and quietly relax. Breath normally and quietly; focus on the in-breath, the pause, the out-breath, the pause. When thoughts arise, acknowledge them and let them pass through your mind like a cloud passes in the sky.

Create a small ball of light in your heart
Focus on the ball of light...
With each breath:
> **Slowly and gently expand the ball of light**
> **until it fills**
> **your body…**
> **the room …**
> **the city …**

the state …
the nation …
the world …
the universe …
all that is …
Allow yourself to feel the vibrant connection
with your loved one
with all that is
Rest in this quiet awareness
Rest in wholeness and connection

Come to this space when you feel lonesome or alone. Come to this space and feel the presence of all your loved ones. Come to this space and understand that you are whole and complete as you are, always connected. The physical world conceals this ever-present holy communion.

To know the truth, we must look beyond what our limited human eyes can see. The truth is we are all connected! WE are all ONE connected in love. We are whole and complete as we are in this very moment. Some moments we know this and some moments we don't. Fortunately, reality is not tied to our knowing or not knowing.

Take a breathing break

Return to life with a positive affirmation

I am ONE with ALL that is

Photo: Cheryl Muck

Practice Session #13: Self-Love

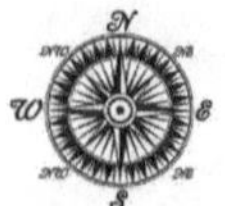

Reading and contemplation

Sometimes it is difficult to love ourselves. We know too much. We focus on our faults instead of our strengths. We hold ourselves to higher standards than we hold others. We rarely show ourselves the same compassion that we would quickly give to a friend.

Practice loving yourself. You will be with yourself all of your life. Others will come and go, but you are your only constant. Do your best to love yourself in an accepting, growing, and compassionate way without being selfish or self-absorbed.

Self-love behaviors:

1. **Be mindful.** Focusing in the present fosters increased happiness. So, you can increase your happiness by learning to live in the here and now with awareness and acceptance of what is. Focusing on the past can lead to depression. When our mind focuses on missed opportunities and "would 'ave, could 'ave, should 'ave" ways of thinking, we are living in the past. Focusing on the future may create anxieties. When we focus on the future, our minds are thinking about the "what ifs" and unknowns of life. Most of us can accept and adjust to changes as they occur in each moment, it is the unknown that is difficult to deal with.
2. **Live with intention.** Our today is the result of all our past choices and actions. Our choices and intentions are the only control we have over our destiny. Take whatever actions lean toward the life you want. We cannot control what happens to us. But we can control how we respond to what happens. Focus your intention on becoming your best self. Water the seeds of happiness and they will grow.
3. **Take care of your body.** We are born with one body and we will have it to the day we die. Practice healthy living — eat and drink to support a healthy body, exercise routinely, sleep

so the body can heal and rest, drink water to hydrate the cells, have routine checkups and preventive tests/treatments.

4. **Create healthy relationships.** Create healthy and supportive relationships. Love and care for your friends without expectation. Welcome the right people into your life. Healthy friends and family accept and love you unconditionally. Establish boundaries and protect yourself from people, places, and activities that deplete you. Say "no" to activities that drain your physical, emotional, or spiritual energy. Let go of any unhealthy automatic behaviors that get you in trouble, keep you stuck in the past, and do not nourish you.
5. **Show yourself compassion.** We can be so hard on ourselves. Learn to forgive yourself when you fall short of being your best self. Accept your humanness. It is good to take responsibility for our decisions and actions. When we learn from mistakes, there are no failures—there are only lessons learned. When we practice self-compassion, we will automatically have enough compassion for others.
6. **Share love.** If you truly love yourself, you will automatically have enough love for others. Love is why we are here. Love is the whole of our purpose. Unconditional love is very powerful. Love yourself unconditionally. Love others unconditionally.

Take a breathing break

Action exercise:

Get up and do a walking meditation. You may not feel like walking or doing anything right now, but you will feel stronger and safer and freer if you do this gentle exercise. If possible go outside to walk. If you cannot go outside, walk quietly and mindfully inside, or even walk in a circle if necessary. Try it! Your body will thank you for it.

Determine how long you want to walk. If walking inside, I recommend at least 10 minutes. If walking outside, I recommend starting with 15 minutes. Set your alarm, so you don't have to watch the clock. If you are walking outside set your alarm for half the time you wish to walk so you can turn around and return on schedule.

Mindful walking is very easy. Simply walk with intention and mindfulness. We usually walk without thinking. In mindful walking, focus your attention on the activity of walking. Feel your feet touch the ground or floor. Feel the movement of your joints and muscles. Feel your arms swinging at your sides. Feel the air gently moving past. Take your time, there is no rush. Nothing to do but walk. Nowhere to go but here. No time to be but now in this walking.

Your mind will wander. That is what minds do. When you notice that your mind has wandered, gently return your thoughts to the walking. No need to be upset or discouraged, simply return to mindful walking.

Some find it easier to focus the mind on a mantra with each step. Simply say a phrase with each step. You may decide to use the affirmation below or another of your choosing. My personal favorite follows: Stepping, I am safe; Stepping, I am loved; Stepping, I am free, repeating as you go. When you notice you are no longer using the affirmation, gently begin again.

Take a breathing break

Return to life with a positive affirmation

I am my own best friend

Practice Session #14: Our Best

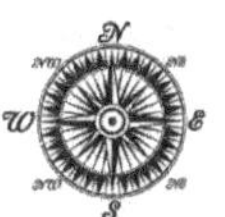

Reading and contemplation

We are all human, perfect in all our imperfections. All we can do is our best at any given time. Our best depends on how we are feeling both physically and emotionally. It helps to remember that our best will vary from time to time and from situation to situation. Our best today will not be the same as yesterday's or tomorrow's best. Since perfection is out of the question our imperfect best is all we have to offer.

At our best:

We care for ourselves.
We are loving and kind.
We strive to see the world from another's point of view.
We take care of others.
We listen with compassionate understanding.
We speak kindly.
We show up and support another in tough times.

We are all human which means we are imperfect.

At less than our best:

We fail to care for ourselves.
We make errors in judgement.
We say things we regret.
We avoid difficult situations.
We neglect actions which might improve outcomes.

Our best is especially needed in trying times and situations. Yet that is when it is most difficult to do our best. Sometimes our best is imperfect. When this happens, mindfully look through the eyes of compassion. With love and generosity, identify the imperfect best in both yourself and others. Accept what is. Choose compassionate understanding over judgement and anger.

Take a breathing break

Action exercise:

Sometimes, we fixate on the times we failed to be our best self. At other times, we generously let go of those efforts that fell short of our best. Our past actions may look inadequate with the knowledge and strengths we possess today. Just as our actions today may look weak with tomorrow's knowledge. All we can do is our best today, in this present moment. Doing our best in the moment helps us avoid self-judgment, self-abuse, and regret. Life is better if we can let go of judgement and accept reality as it is. May we each learn to care more and judge less.

Today, right now, take 15 minutes and write a gratitude note to someone you care about. Tell them how grateful you are that they are in your life. Describe something specific they said or did that was their best. Let them know that you appreciate them.

Take a breathing break

Return to life with a positive affirmation

Today I am being my best self

Practice Session #15: Guilt

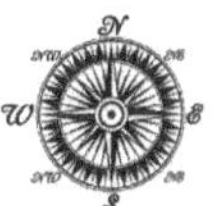

Reading and contemplation

There is the potential for guilt in every day, in every moment, in every action and in every relationship. No one is perfect. There is always something better that we could have done or said. Unhealthy guilt is based in the past; it is all about being in a state of would ‘ave, could ‘ave, should ‘ave.

Release your guilt. Let it go. Ruminating on what you could have done differently serves no purpose. Did all the time you spent with your dying friend not matter just because you weren’t there at the moment of their death? Perhaps you think your loved one didn’t know you loved them, simply because you never said it the last time you spoke. Let go of all the past imperfections. The past is gone, learn from it. Learn from each lesson, and then gently let it go.

The best way to avoid unhealthy guilt is to stay grounded in this moment. Today, here and now, we can accept our past and understand that we all fall short of our highest expectations. When we get mired down in guilt, we stop the natural learning, growth and change that arises from our imperfections. The best way to honor the past is to be your best self today.

Lay down the burden of an imperfect past. You did the best you could in that time and situation. It may not have been as good as you would have liked, but it was what you were capable of in that moment. Let go of all that could have been different and accept what was. Focus instead on what is in this moment and mindfully be your best self today.

Take a breathing break

Action exercise:

Take out a piece of paper. Consider your loss and grief. Make a list of everything about which you feel guilty. Write down all your regrets (stream of consciousness) without judgement or evaluation. Write until you have no more guilt ridden regrets to list.

Study each item on the list. Ask these questions:

1. Could I have done better—under those specific circumstances, in that place and at that time?

a. If not, let it go. You did your best. Stop beating yourself up. You may hope to do things different or better next time. Do not allow that to stop you from accepting that you did your best under the circumstances at that point in time. Next time you will be more experienced and wiser, so your best may be different.

b. *ACTION:* Sometimes, especially when you are having trouble letting go of regret or guilt, it may be helpful to take some action to release the guilt. Some examples are: writing it all down (journaling), creating a totem to hold the guilt and get rid of it (burning ritual/ceremony, shredding it), discussing with a trusted friend, etc. Do whatever works for you to let it go.

2. Did I cause harm or pain to anyone besides myself?

a. Make a list of anyone who you think you might have hurt as a result of your loss and grief. Can I do anything that will make amends for this wrong I did to another?

b. *ACTION:* Make amends, unless doing so would harm them or another. If you can't make amends today, write down a plan to make amends. Keep your plan with your calendar until the list is completed.

i. Plan the details including who, when, where and how you will make amends. Better yet, do it now.

ii. Call, meet, or write a letter/card to this person.

iii. Tell them your concerns about not doing your best. Let them know you are sorry for any pain you may have caused them and that you hope to do better in the future.

iv. Tell them you want to move forward together toward

a better tomorrow.

Take a breathing break

Return to life with a positive affirmation

I assume responsibility for my actions

Photo: Cheryl Muck

Practice Session #16: Impermanence

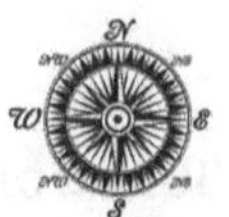

Reading and contemplation

Life seems to be easier when we see it as an ever-changing process. This is a more accurate view of reality. Adapting to changing circumstances may be one of life's hardest lessons. When we resist change, we resist the very nature of our existence and the reality we live within. And yet, we continue to want things and people and places to stay the same, secure and safe.

Sometimes life changes gradually giving us time to adapt and adjust. At other times our world completely changes in the blink of an eye. In that instant, we are suddenly fish out of water, struggling for our very survival.

Some changes we tend to label as good—the longed-for pregnancy occurs, the love of our life is found, the perfect job offer arrives, the cure is found. Some changes we tend to label as bad—a love is lost, the terminal diagnosis is identified, the horrible accident occurs, a disability takes over, the loved one dies.

We hold on to the past. We dream of going back. We mourn for what was. This is a normal response to loss and change. Sometimes we discover that things we thought were forever lost have really only changed. Over time, we learn that the time we spent with a loved one still continues to shape and change us as we move forward. They are never really gone from our life. The ripples of our time together remain with us always.

Ultimately, accepting the truth of impermanence is critical to our happiness. When we hold on to the past, we can miss the joy of being fully present in this moment, here and now. No matter how hard we try, joy can never be experienced in the past or in the future. Joy can be remembered from the past or hoped for in the future. Yet, joy can only be experienced in the current moment. We are on the path to recovery when we begin to feel deep gratitude for the past and also release it to mindfully experience the present moment.

Take a breathing break

Action exercise:

Once you feel peaceful and relaxed, close your eyes and contemplate the life of a flower.

THE SEED,
the warm earth,
the lovely rain,
the sunshine,
the sprouting,
the fresh growth,
the budding,
the full bloom,
the fragrance,
the bees,
the pollination,
the seeds falling,
the wilting,
the collapse,
the decomposing,
the nourishing earth,
THE SEED
the cycle of life
without complaint or strife.
forever changing and
forever remaining,
and so it goes.

Photo: Cheryl Muck

Take a breathing break

Return to life with a positive affirmation

I accept the reality of impermanence

Photo: Cheryl Muck

Photo: Cheryl Muck

Practice Session #17: Resiliency

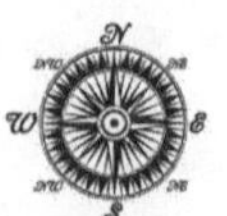

Reading and contemplation

If you are experiencing loss and grief, you are probably not feeling very resilient. Even though I may not know you, I know that you are stronger than you think and have resources available to help you. Use your resources during this time of loss and grief. Everyone needs help getting through hard times.

We are not born resilient. Rather, as we live, we learn to be resilient. This means we can take actions and make decisions that support resilience. Everyone can benefit from learning to be more resilient. There are local counselors and resources on the internet if you want help developing resiliency skills.

Research has identified personal qualities that build resiliency. The following action exercise outlines a list of Individual Qualities that Facilitate Resiliency developed by Nan Henderson, M.S.W. We each have our own strengths which support our resiliency. Which resiliency characteristics do you possess?

Everyone has their own way of dealing with loss, crisis, stress, and trauma. Use the skills which have helped you get through previous difficult times. Arm yourself with every resiliency tool you can develop. Your entire life will be happier for it!

Take a breathing break

Action exercise:

Go online and search the resiliency quiz at www.resiliency.com. Take the resiliency quiz. Review the Resiliency list developed by Nan Henderson, M.S.W. Truthfully evaluate which qualities you already possess. Think about your personal experiences, character and strengths.

- **Relationships**
- **Service**
- **Humor**
- **Inner Direction**
- **Perceptiveness**
- **Independence**
- **Positive View of Personal Future**
- **Flexibility**
- **Love of Learning**
- **Self-motivation**
- **Competence**
- **Self-worth**
- **Spirituality**
- **Perseverance**
- **Creativity**

List your resiliency characteristics on a note card and carry it with you to pull out when you are feeling overwhelmed. Focus on your current 3 - 5 greatest strengths and use them to boost your resilience through grief. Make a concrete plan for how to use those strengths to help you survive and even thrive.

If you enjoy reading, get a copy of *The Tao of Pooh* by Benjamin Hoff. What a wonderful fun book this is! It supports being your best self, like the quote, "Promise me you'll always remember: You're braver than you believe, and stronger than you seem, and smarter than you think."

Take a breathing break

Return to life with a positive affirmation

I am resilient

Practice Session #18: Special Occasions

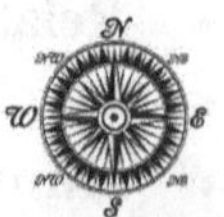

Reading and Contemplation

Most of us look forward to special occasions and celebrations. Holidays, birthdays, anniversaries have very individual meanings to each of us. Rituals and traditions give meaning and depth to our common life experiences. They express our humanity and help us feel part of a group. Those meanings and feelings do not disappear when someone leaves our life.

After a loss, each special occasion can create a new sense of grief and separation. The first year is full of adjustments and changes and new firsts. Special occasions remind us of our loss as memories of our life before come up. Sometimes a tradition we never liked suddenly becomes important, or another ritual we previously loved no longer has meaning. Each situation and event needs to be considered, and decisions on what to do have to be made. It can be overwhelming.

Mindfully planning holidays can lead to better outcomes, happier events, and stronger ties with family and friends. One key to success is to honestly talk to all those involved before making special occasion decisions.

There are really only three choices in the end; the rest is just details. The event goes on as usual. The event goes on with some planned modifications. The event changes entirely. Talk about it; make a decision and do the best you can. It will be enough. Remember there are no good or bad decisions. Each situation has its own answer.

In the end, we may decide to mindfully make decisions, or we may choose to avoid and ignore the event. The holiday will come with or without our plans. The special occasions and holidays will arrive, on schedule, as they always have. You, your family and friends will survive. New events and new rituals will arise and gain importance until they fade.

Learn to be mindfully present in each special occasion and holiday. The JOY is in being mindfully present during the event.

Take a breathing break

Action exercise:

Take a few minutes and write down all the special celebrations and traditions you have created with the person you lost. List the family and friends that were also involved in each of those traditions. Now take a few minutes and think about what you want to do or change for each of those traditions/celebrations. Then, note if you would like to discard, enjoy or change this tradition.

Make a plan to discuss those ideas with the relevant family and friends. Thoughtfully and gently discuss and decide what to keep, what to let go, and what new traditions to start. When changing a tradition, think about anything you are doing new and take some action to make it memorable and special. That is how the old traditions started. Traditions are that simple. Someone first made the effort to make an event special and memorable.

Do what works best for you and your given or chosen family. Each individual and group is different, and one solution will not meet everyone's needs. Each new milestone and event will come, be experienced, and move into the past. Trying to avoid or ignore the special occasion is not really a viable option; time always marches on and memories pop into our minds unbidden. Regardless of what you decide, the first year will be different and for most people challenging. If we take actions to plan special occasions, it may help everyone deal with changed traditions after loss.

Take a breathing break

Return to life with a positive affirmation

I choose which traditions to discard or enjoy or change

Photo: Michael Smith

Practice Session #19: Patience

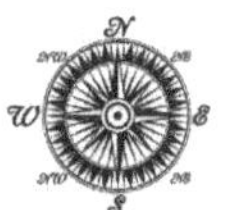

Reading and Contemplation

No one is born patient. It is a skill we can learn over a lifetime. It is easiest to practice with the little things in life. That way when the big things come along, we are already skilled in patience.

Recovering from loss and grief requires a considerable amount of patience. Some approaches that strengthen patience are outlined below. Impatience is difficult to identify early before it grows out of control. When the first sense of impatience arises, try to step back to observe the situation, breathe slowly, and determine how to acknowledge and move beyond your impatience.

- **Identify when feelings of impatience arise.** Impatience usually starts with strong feelings like anger, fear, irritation, blaming and shaming. It can be focused outward toward others. Or it can be focused inward toward ourselves. Instead of raging at some event over which you have no control, learn to mentally step back and observe what is happening. We become happier when we learn to identify and observe strong negative feelings before they blow out of control. Impatience is not about the situation, it is always about our response to the situation.
- **Allow the experience of discomfort and pain.** We sometimes desire only pleasure, comfort and acceptance. Yet, life is full of feelings which come and go continually. Enjoy positive feelings when they arise and know they will soon pass away. When less desirable feelings arise, simply acknowledge them and let them pass. Acknowledge impatience (or any emotion) when it occurs and then decide how to respond. Cultivating patience will support clarity and the ability to deal with whatever is causing pain or discomfort.
- **Stop the chatter box from running with a storyline.** We fuel our emotions (like impatience) when we create a story around our feelings. Sometimes, it is easier to develop a storyline than

simply be present with what is going on in our lives. Unfortunately, our chatter box tends to focus on negative issues. If we create a storyline we amplify the negative results.

- **Practice being patient and kind with yourself.** Instead of being upset with yourself for having negative feelings, be patient and show yourself kindness. Try some positive self-talk. How about, "My life is hard right now; it will not always be so. I am dealing with loss and grief. My response is natural and healthy. I don't like going through this, but I will heal with time."

When struggling with the jagged road of grief, remember the words of William Shakespeare:

> "How poor are they that have not patience!
> What wound did ever heal but by degree?"

Take a breathing break

Action exercise:

Spend a few minutes contemplating impatience. Ask yourself these questions:

- Is impatience an issue in my life?
- Do I want to decrease my impatience tendencies?
- What can I learn about myself by understanding my moments of impatience?

How can we decrease impatience?

- Try identifying impatience early when it arises.
- Try simply observing impatience without any judgement or action.
- Try letting go of the illusion of control.
- Try practicing tolerance and simply allow things to be as they are.
- Try using the serenity prayer.

"God grant me the serenity to accept the things I cannot change, the courage to change the things I can and the wisdom to know the difference." Reinhold Niebuhr

Take a breathing break

Return to life with a positive affirmation

I am patient with life - just as it is

Practice Session #20: Living Now

Reading and Contemplation

Loss and grief can throw us into a time warp. It is painful to be present with the loss. It is challenging to live here and now. Sometimes it is simply easier to escape to a rosy past or the greener grass of the future.

It can also be pleasant to reflect on the past and keep our loved one with us by reliving times spent together. We may see the world through the eyes of our lost loved one instead of using our own eyes. We may see the past through rose-colored or regret-colored glasses. An appropriate honest life review and reflection is good. However, too much focus on the past can lead to depression.

Making plans for the future is healthy and necessary, but making big changes are probably not wise while grieving. Grief can create an inaccurate point of view when we try to imagine the future. We may not be able to envision the life changes our loss will create. We may think our future is unmanageable without the lost one. Focusing too much on the future can easily lead to anxiety. It may be helpful to stay focused in the present and allow the future to evolve naturally over time.

Healing is supported when we stay in the present moment. Healing happens one day at a time. Be with the loss and grief. Survive today and discover that life does go on. Laughter happens again. Maybe not today, but soon. Being with the grief today lays the foundation for a whole and healthy life tomorrow.

If you have suffered a great loss, your life will not be the same. You will be forever changed. By making changes toward good, it is still possible to give meaning and purpose to loss. Love more. Appreciate every moment. Live deeper. Spread joy. Enjoy every precious moment.

Take a breathing break

Action exercise:

We each have the ability to choose one thought over another. We can all use the breath to center, calm and comfort the body. Practicing our focused breathing helps us be mindful and present in the current moment.

With practice, it becomes easier to return to the NOW. Anyone can do it. Simply focus your awareness on the breath. Pay attention to the cycle of the breath. Breathe in, pause; breathe out, pause; and repeat. Focus your full undivided attention on the breath.

At some point, you will recognize that your mind has wandered. This is natural and happens to everyone. Without judgement, gently focus your mind back on the breath. Breathe in, pause; breathe out, pause; and repeat. With practice, this focused attention on the breath gets easier.

And yet, on any given day (especially when stressed or distracted), it is easy to lose focus. Be kind to yourself when you lose focus. Do not judge or focus on the distraction. Simply smile, acknowledge the wandering mind, and return to the breath. Stay focused on the breath with your full undivided attention.

As you go through your daily routine, stop and practice your breathing exercise for a few minutes. It is very helpful when you feel stress or anxiety rising up. It is usually easier to do before you feel overwhelmed. This simple exercise engages your body's normal relaxation response. And the good news is no special equipment or skills are needed! Your breath is always with you and ready to help you relax! Your body's relaxation response gets stronger with use, just like exercising a muscle. The more you practice, the easier it will be to engage your natural relaxation response.

Take a breathing break

Return to life with a positive affirmation

I live in the present moment

Photo: Cheryl Muck

Practice Session #21: Stuff

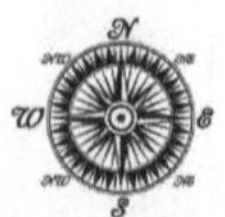

Reading and Contemplation

It can be difficult to deal with all the accumulated stuff a loved one collected — a life time of clothes, books, memorabilia, art, knick-knacks, tools, pictures, the list goes on. At some point, if you are in control of the assets, you have to deal with all the stuff. There is no right or wrong way, no time-line to do this. It is difficult to let go of the things your loved one no longer needs. Think about what feels right for you. Make a plan, make a schedule, and then stop thinking about it. Just do it.

Discarding stuff that belonged to a loved one is very difficult and may be one of the most painful things you ever do. You don't have to do it alone. Some find that doing it with someone else helps ease the pain. At the same time, it can also be cathartic to let go of all the stuff. Most likely you will have mixed feelings. Just remember, getting rid of your loved one's possessions does not mean you are getting rid of your memories or of the love you carry in your heart.

On the other hand, the *stuff* could be memorabilia you are holding onto. You may not be in charge of the belongings of the person you lost (to death or estrangement). This does not mean that you don't have to deal with an accumulation of stuff related to your lost love. The loss still exists, and the difficult task still needs to be done.

Today's action exercise is about developing a strategy and planning a schedule for dealing with the all that stuff. According to where you are in the grieving process you may still have lots or very little with which to deal. Regardless, it probably can't be done in a day.

Take a breathing break

Action exercise:

Think about the ideas below and take action on dealing with any stuff hanging over your head. Consider these examples and use whatever strategy works for you or make up your own strategy.

- Take pictures of the things and memorabilia that had meaning to your loved one or to you. Make an album or create a picture book to hold those memories. Usually we keep stuff to retain the attached memories. Those memories can be invoked with a picture as easily as the thing itself. You don't have to keep all the things around you to recall the memories. In fact, all the stuff can get lost and not even be seen in the background of our lives.

- Ask close friends and family if there is anything they would like. Whenever possible include all family members; it is amazing how many people hold scars from how a loved-one's personal possessions were distributed by another. I have talked with families that held that anger over generations. Step lovingly, speak kindly, involve anyone that needs to be involved. No amount of stuff is worth creating family pain that can last generations.

- If it helps, have a relative or friend help you sort through the clothes and other possessions. It is OK to keep things for yourself. If you will use it or it will bring you comfort, keep it until it no longer serves that function. Trash what is worn out. Donate the clothes, shoes, accessories that can be used by someone in need.

- If you can't release something yet, pack it up and store it. Put a note on your calendar for a date to pull out the box and determine if you are ready to release the items. This gives you time to decide what to keep while also moving you forward. You may love getting items out years later and telling stories about them and the departed loved one.

- Think about the future before getting rid of all the stuff. There will be special events and milestones where items might be used as very special gifts. Grandma's special Christmas dishes might make the perfect wedding gift for a grandchild. Grandpa's pocket knife or work tools might be a great graduation gift for a grandson. Woodworking tools might make the special retirement gift for a friend. Select, box and store items to keep for future occasions. Keep a list and pictures of the stored items.

- Donate all items that might be of value to another. Do it with a generous heart, knowing that another can benefit.

Take a breathing break

Return to life with a positive affirmation

My loved one will always be in my life

Practice Session #22: Allow Healing

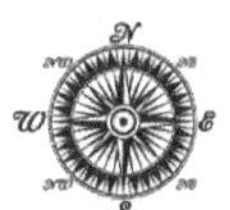

Reading and Contemplation

Healing takes time. Give yourself the gift of time to heal. Be patient with your healing process. Consciously do things to help yourself heal. Follow your heart, it knows best when it comes to healing. The mind can distract or lead you astray.

No one will ever replace your past love. They will always be with you. Anyone, anything, anyplace you have truly loved becomes a part of you. Love relationships never end. The relationship changes when we are physically separated. And yet, our relationship remains and continues to impact all that we are and do. A dear friend, years gone, impacts a decision today. A mother's love gives us the will to go on for our own children. The strength of our father allows us to stand up to discrimination. The love of a spouse teaches us to love ourselves. The bad relationship impacts our future relationships.

If we love, we cannot avoid loss and suffering. Along with pain and suffering, there is also goodness and joy in the world. Learn to anticipate and celebrate all the goodness and joy. Let your life unfold even amidst the grief of lost love.

Over time current relationships will change and new relationships may form. A dear friend may love you unconditionally, as did your lost mother. A boss or co-worker may believe in you as only your father did before. A young neighbor may become your outlet for mentoring. A new love might appear. Each relationship will be different, not better or worse, just different. Keep your heart open for new opportunities to share life and love. Love takes many forms. Open your heart to love wherever it is found.

Healing and allowing yourself to move on is respectful of the lost love. You are not being unfaithful to your loved one. If they ever truly loved you, they want your happiness. If you truly loved them, you know the joy of sharing life with another.

Take the seeds of your lost dreams and love and plant them where they might bloom again when spring comes. Celebrate the sun, the warmth, the rain. Anticipate the blossoming as a tribute to your lost love.

Take a breathing break

Action exercise:

Set your phone alarm for 10 - 15 minutes. Get up and take a mindful walk. This can happen inside or out. Walk mindfully. Stay aware of each step, each breath. If it helps you stay present, take a step with each breath in and each breath out. If focusing on both is difficult, focus on your steps and breath normally. Stay focused on this moment. Here and now.

When you realize your mind has wandered, bring it back to this moment. Walk mindfully. Breath mindfully. Stay aware of each step, each breath. Focus on the feeling of touching the floor, the earth; focus on the sensation of the breath coming and going. Be present in this moment. Let go of the past and stop projecting into the future. Just be present in this moment. Here and now.

To increase your focus, try coordinating your walking with a mantra (sounds or words used to focus concentration). Three of my favorite walking mantras are below.

Step 1 - I am safe;
Step 2 - I am loved;
Step 3 - I am free.

Repeat through walking time.

Step 1 - I have arrived,

step 2 - I am home.

Repeat through walking time.

Step 1 - Here,
Step 2 - Now.

Repeat through walking time.

As you walk, continue bringing your mind back to the present. Mindfulness is like a muscle that strengthens with use. It requires practice to learn to be present and mindful in each moment. Healing occurs in this moment, right now. We cannot heal in the past or the future. Healing can only happen now, in this moment. Support your healing by being present where healing can occur.

Take a breathing break

Return to life with a positive affirmation

I take the time I need to heal

Practice Session #23: Jagged Road

Reading and contemplation

If you are on a healing journey, think of it as the jagged road. Healing is not a straight-line journey ever upward. It is a jagged road—up and down, left and right, forward and backward. Trust that healing is happening, whether or not you know it. The healing process can be especially messy if we try to ignore or avoid it. Honor your journey down the jagged road of grief. It is the only road to the other side. Allow healing at your own pace.

Most of the time we expect everything at the speed of the internet. We have no patience. We don't understand why we feel worse today than yesterday, or this morning, or before. We feel discouraged when we think we regress or backslide. When this happens, simply notice the self-critic at work; ask that mean critic to stand down and cut you some slack. Take a moment and practice your favorite breathing exercise. Focus on your breath until calm arrives. Remember the healing process is a messy, jagged road that must be traversed. Self-criticism at this time is not helpful.

We sometimes have friends or family that want us to progress at the pace they believe is right. Trust yourself; remember you are the best judge of your own healing. You do not have to understand or accept the loss on someone else's schedule. The process is different for everyone, so be authentic to your own needs. Your healing process may be delayed if you artificially shrug off your loss and grief to meet someone else's schedule.

Be patient with yourself and be patient with those who want you to move faster. On the other hand, if you are not progressing according to what your heart tells you is right, do not hesitate to get expert help. Seek out a counselor specializing in loss and grief or a local grief support group. Your local hospice will have expert knowledge regarding the local resources available for grief recovery.

The healing process continually trends upward in spite of its jagged nature. The road will become straighter. The mountains and valleys will level out. The sun will shine again.

Take a breathing break

Action exercise:

Some find it easier to speak truths and share their story with others not living through the same loss. Below are some steps which will help you find grief recovery support in your local area. Take notes on what you find or print out local resource information.

1. Contact your physician or local hospices for references on counselors specializing in loss and grief.
2. Google hospice and your location to find area hospices. Most hospices have routine bereavement activities and are welcoming to all. Call and see what services they offer.
3. Conduct an internet search using your location and grief recovery support groups. Contact the groups to determine their support services.
4. Most local areas of any size also have specialty support groups for widows/widowers, parents, specific diseases/conditions, suicide loss, Mothers Against Drunk Driving, etc. Sometimes sharing with someone that has a similar loss can be especially meaningful.

Call today and find out what is available in your area. Take action if you feel it will benefit your journey.

Take a breathing break

Return to life with a positive affirmation

I accept the ups and downs of my grief process

Photo: Cheryl Muck

Practice Session #24: Accepting Kindness

Reading and Contemplation

Many people will show kindness to us when we experience loss and grief. Take all of it in. Accept the love and compassion being given. Giving has curative power for both the recipient and the giver. We all need compassion from time to time, but it can be hard to relax and accept.

Most of us are more comfortable giving kindness than accepting it for ourselves. If that is true for you, remember that accepting a kindness returns a kindness to the giver. When bad things happen, it is painful for everyone around. Most people struggle with what to do and what to say. Showing benevolence may be their only outlet for compassion.

When a recipient graciously accepts thoughtfulness, there is a measure of healing for all involved. Both parties become more isolated when the recipient rejects or demeans a kindness. So, learn to graciously accept acts of kindness. Experience the compassionate moment with joy and love. Allow kindness to wash over you. Allow love and compassion to wash away some of the hurt in this moment.

When we share little kindnesses, we embrace the truth of our common humanity. We are our best selves. A thoughtfulness shared gives us all hope for the future.

Take a breathing break

Action exercise:

When we look with our big mind
we all know the truth

There is no giver
There is no receiver

There is only giving
There is only receiving

The universe ebbing
The universe flowing

Take a breathing break

Return to life with a positive affirmation

I accept kindness

Practice Session #25: Giving Kindness

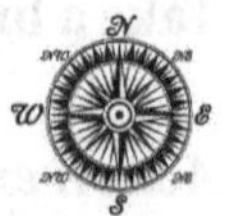

Reading and Contemplation

When we experience loss and grief, it is easy to get caught up in our own problems. We tend to see the world through our own pain. Our vision becomes distorted. We can easily become so involved in our own story that we forget there are others in pain. Remember on any given day 5 to 10 percent of the people you encounter will be in the first year of grieving for a family member.

There are many people in need of help, compassion, and understanding. Do something kind for another; it will probably bring you a sense of joy and meaning. When we act out of love and connection with no expectations, we naturally feel better. Service takes us out of ourselves and helps us see beyond our own problems.

Service is the manifestation of compassion. It is the doing tied to compassion. Balance the giving and accepting of kindness during your grief. Compassion for our common humanity brings some relief as long as we do not use it to overshadow our experience of the pain of loss.

Take a breathing break

Action exercise:

There are many opportunities in life to be of service to others. Any act of kindness and love is a moment of service. Notice and help others in need. Open your eyes and ears to see and hear when someone needs your assistance. Don't offer to do something - just do it. Take action to help another on their journey.

One of my favorite little books is *Random Acts of Kindness* by The Editors of Conari Press (Author), Dawna Markova (Introduction), Daphne Rose Kingma (Foreword), copyright 1993. My copy was published in 2002. If you do an internet search on the title, you will find an entire world of books, gifts, cards and resources related to random acts of kindness. It is uplifting just to browse through the information. Google "Random Acts of Kindness" and browse the offerings.

A random act of kindness is an unplanned and unpredictable action done for no reason but to offer kindness towards the outside world. The phrase "practice random kindness and senseless acts of beauty" was written by Anne Herbert on a placemat in Sausalito, CA in 1982. This small act started a massive movement which has its own annual international day each February. You can join that movement today. Experience the joy of giving kindness and love to the world.

Research shows that the very act of doing a kindness for someone else releases feel-good chemicals into our body. In fact, the chemicals are stronger when we do a kind act than if someone does a kindness for us. So, an act of kindness helps you as much, if not more, than the one you serve.

TODAY look for an opportunity to do a kindness. Don't make it too difficult or take too much time to consider it. Just do it. Take action to share a random act of kindness with someone you know or a total stranger. When you consciously choose to do a random act of kindness, it will brighten your day.

Take a breathing break

Return to life with a positive affirmation

I routinely give kindness

Practice Session #26: Forgiving Others

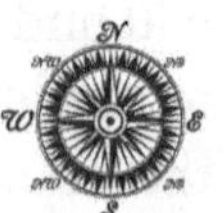

Reading and Contemplation

We all fail to be our best selves from time to time. Each of us have said or done things that hurt others. Sometimes we know it, but many times we do not even recognize the hurt we have caused. We know this is true. When it comes to our own hurts, we tend to take it personally. We believe someone purposefully wronged and hurt us. In reality, they are probably just having a less than perfect moment. We create a personal story line by building scenarios in our minds about how we were hurt or treated unfairly. Over time our hurts and resentments build up and become a heavy load we carry around every moment. We can start seeing each life interaction through our filter of hurt and resentment, adding to our specific victim story line.

Forgiveness is all about letting go of actual and perceived past hurts. Dropping the heavy load of past resentments allows us to live a lighter and happier life. Forgiveness is founded on the insight that all people are worthy of our love and compassion, no exceptions. All fall short of perfection and nevertheless remain worthy. Forgiveness helps us overcome the pain and the bitterness of living with negative memories. Forgiving does not mean we forget or condone the act or perceived injustice. Forgiveness means we release its hold on our life. It allows us to move forward without malice, anger, or the desire for revenge.

When we lose someone, there may be opportunities to practice forgiveness. Forgiveness requires that we first acknowledge and understand how we were harmed by another. This can be hard. Sometimes, when we have been hurt by a loved one, we find it difficult to acknowledge their flaws. When we accept the truth of both the good and bad in our relationships and loved ones, we are freed to forgive and see our past as it truly was. Simply accept that our relationship was perfect in all its imperfections. We are who and what and where we are today because of all that has come before, even the painful bits.

We are always free to forgive. We are the only one with the power to forgive another or even ourselves. We each have the power to release ourselves from the past and live freely in the present. So, when we can, we forgive, not for the others but for ourselves. Old hurts and resentments will continue to arise until we release them through active forgiveness. Without forgiveness, we can remain stuck in past resentments and anger. Forgiveness takes time. It is not a one-and-done activity but a continual lifetime practice. We can experience the relief of releasing past hurts. We can mindfully lay down past hurts and resentments. We may also choose to forgive ourselves for judging another. Our hearts naturally soar when released from hurt, anger and resentment.

Take a breathing break

Action exercise:

Be present in this moment and allow the past to float by like a cloud in the sky. While you are relaxed and peaceful, take positive action by offering forgiveness to another and yourself. Use the following examples to create an individualized statement for your circumstances.

> I forgive John for not taking better care of himself
> and I forgive myself for judging his behaviors and nagging him.
>
> I forgive my sister for not being there for mom
> and I forgive myself for judging her behavior.

Repeat the forgiveness statement as many times as necessary to fully release your resentments and anger. Say it out loud! Forgiveness creates a foundation for healing. Come back to this exercise and peel this onion until you are finished with the guilt and anger and resentment.

Some words of caution: Forgiveness is a private event.

It is not helpful to verbalize forgiveness unless the offender requests it. The offender may not even perceive that they need to be forgiven. In fact, unsolicited forgiveness is nearly always perceived as a threat or attack. Forgiveness is best left as a private event. Forgiveness is really not about another anyway. We forgive another to resolve and dissipate our resentment and anger toward them. The higher road is to privately forgive and treat the offender with unconditional love. Allow your actions to speak for you. Hostilities nearly always disappear in the face of true unconditional love.

Asking for another's forgiveness is basically a self-focused and manipulative action. A better approach is to name what you feel you did wrong, and tell them how you hope to do better next time. "I'm sorry" helps another. "Please forgive me" remains all about you.

Take a breathing break

Return to life with a positive affirmation

I forgive ___ for ___ and
I forgive myself for judging ___

Practice Session #27: Forgiving Ourselves

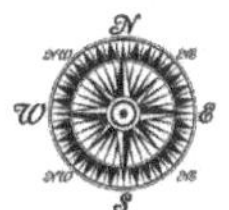

Reading and Contemplation

The sooner you can forgive yourself the better. Yes, you will most likely need to forgive yourself! Remember we are all imperfect. There are probably actions, words, feelings, mistakes, or offenses which you believe created or hastened your loss. You may feel like it was your fault. You may feel you did something to create pain for the lost one. You may think you could have done something to change this awful outcome. Feelings of guilt almost always accompany loss and grief.

These beliefs may or may not be reality based. It does not matter; forgive yourself. Forgive yourself for being human and making human mistakes. Forgive yourself for judging yourself. Forgive yourself for not letting go of the past. Forgive yourself for moving on and living your life without your loved one. Forgive yourself for being less than perfect.

Love yourself enough to forgive yourself. Choose to make a fresh start. Choose to go on living a full and happy life. Love yourself unconditionally!

Take a breathing break

Action exercise:

Take a few minutes to settle into this moment, right now. Relax your body. Starting at the top of your head - relax your scalp, breath; relax your eyes, breath; relax your jaw, breath; relax your shoulders, breathe; relax your arms and hands, breathe; relax your back, breathe; relax your butt, breathe; relax your thighs, breathe; relax your calves, breathe; relax your feet, breathe. Sit in this relaxed state until you feel light and free. Once you are completely relaxed, do the exercise below. You can do both or pick one. Do whatever seems most helpful. It is best if you write the letter out in longhand as handwriting uses a different more creative part of your brain than typing.

Write a letter to your younger self.

Pick a critical point in time that you feel needs self-forgiveness. Write the letter in the present tense, e.g.: "I am so proud of who you are! You are stronger than you think. You will get through this tough time."

- Start by remembering details of the critical point in time
- Tell your younger self how much you are loved
- Review what is going on in your younger life
- Let your younger self know how sorry you are that these events are happening
- Acknowledge any decisions or actions that need forgiveness
- Forgive your younger self for any imperfect actions or decisions
- Thank your younger self for getting you to where you are today

Write a letter from the future to yourself now.

Pick a time maybe 10 to 20 years from now. Take a few minutes to clearly visualize yourself in the future.

Where are you? What have you learned? Who have you become? What advice do you want to give yourself?

Take a breathing break

Return to life with a positive affirmation

I love myself without conditions

Photo: Michael Smith

Practice Session #26: Blameless

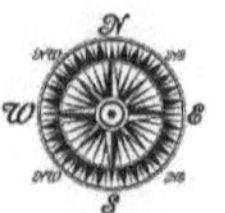

Reading and Contemplation

We humans try to make sense of the world. We want to believe there is a reason for everything. Our minds tend to make up connections and causes where none exist. Sometimes we even turn our illogical musings into superstitions. Even though we know that the very nature of life is temporary, we might blame ourselves, the person we lost, someone else, or God for a loss or death.

We can blame ourselves for the loss. We can blame the victim for actions which led to their death or their departure from our life. We might blame someone else for taking away a loved one. When we assign blame, we are fighting against the very nature of humankind. We all make mistakes. We all fall short of perfect behavior. We all die.

For the most part—we cannot control what happens to us. The only thing we can control is how we respond. Trying to assign blame for loss or grief is a fruitless adventure. You are blameless. They are blameless. God is blameless. Don't get stuck in the blame game. Accept what has happened as much as possible and be at peace with what is. Lean into the future and accept life as ever-changing. Most of the time life is good, and sometimes it is bad. See loss and grief in context of life's entirety. When we love, sooner or later, we either experience loss or create loss for another. In deciding to love, we also decide love is worth it. We make that decision, and there is no one to blame. We open our heart and our arms to another. Ultimately, that is always a good thing!

Change and loss and death and grief are normal events experienced by every human being. They are normal emotions that come and pass away if we allow. We can keep memories and love alive while letting go of pain and blame. Allow yourself to accept loss and grief as normal events in life. Let go of blame, forgive everyone and be open to happiness. Love and life always wins over loss and grief. We can live now. We can let go of our past pain and lean into tomorrow unafraid. Life can be difficult, and it certainly is not always fair. It can also be beautiful and filled with joy. Focusing energy and time on blaming keeps us absorbed with the past. When we move forward past blame we experience a brighter present moment, here and now.

Take a breathing break

Action exercise:

Harold S. Kushner, in *When Bad Things Happen to Good People*, does a wonderful job of helping us let go of BLAME and live into our reality. He helps us understand that we will all face loss and suffer. He suggests that blaming or asking "why" may be the wrong question. The better question when bad things happen is, "What do I do now that this has happened?"

Set your alarm for 10 minutes. Relax and sit quietly while you do the following contemplative meditation.

Contemplate the blame and fault-finding reactions you experience related to loss and grief. Consider who you blame for your losses. As you think of each person, hold him/her in your heart and visualize getting down on your knees and bathing their feet in loving acceptance. Allow any blame you feel to wash away into the ocean for cleansing. Accept that no one, including yourself, is responsible for your loss.

Take a breathing break

Return to life with a positive affirmation

I am in control of my response to life

Practice Session #29: Stories

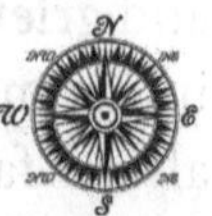

Reading and Contemplation

Sometimes, we build drama and create stories around our personal lives, especially when we experience loss. Our minds can turn anyone into other than what they were. Our lost husband might morph into the greatly missed handyman that he never was in reality. Our difficult child can become loving and respectful and full of great potential. Our dear friend becomes closer and more meaningful in her death than she ever was in life. Our mother becomes the saint. Our lost love turns into our one and only soul mate.

Grief can distort reality. It is normal and natural, especially in the initial stages of grief, to see only the positive and good about the lost one. At some point, it is also natural to let the drama and stories go. When we accurately identify and accept the flaws of our lost one, it supports accurate memories and a better understanding of humanity. Rejoicing in our shared life and happy times gives meaning to our lost relationship. It can be wonderful to embrace and appreciate memories that accurately reflect reality. Accurately seeing our loved one and remembering our life together helps us heal and live in truth today.

Acknowledging our loss and accepting reality helps us move forward. Holding onto drama and stories can keep us locked in the past and our current grief, unable to move forward with our life. Understanding past relationships can positively influence our current relationships and life. Amazingly, there can be a solemn beauty and majesty to grief. From time to time, we see the emergence of the sparkling diamond of a new self. That glimmer can give us a moment of sheer joy and wonder. When this happens, allow yourself to enjoy the moment! This is natural. You are growing. You are changing. It is good. You are a diamond emerging from the crushing pressure of grief.

Take a breathing break

Action exercise:

Most of the time our lives seem stable and permanent. In reality, our lives are more like a long vacation with an end date always approaching. Each day is precious and special, and once lived we will never get it back. We can engage in life, or we can be a spectator. We can choose to take it all in, or we can put up barriers and play it safe. We can fog through life or live mindfully in each moment. Regardless of how we choose to live, we experience both pain and joy.

Living mindfully is the best way to learn how to savor life and experience more joy without drama or stories. It is really simple. You already know how to live mindfully. You naturally did it as a child, until you learned how to worry about tomorrow and judge yesterday. According to Jesus, one way to enter the kingdom of heaven is to become like a little child. Even today, the joy of the kingdom can be seen in the innocent face of a child fully engaged in the moment. Anyone can recapture that awe and wonder and joy. Simply let go of the past and the future. Be present, here and now, in this moment. Be aware of everything. Try it. Live in the moment, be present with whatever is happening in this moment. If you can live even one hour in pure mindfulness, the JOY will overwhelm you. With all the pain of life, there is still much joy.

Today, focus on becoming aware of things, places, nature, feelings, anything encountered! Be present with what is rather than creating a story of pain or persecution. Be present with what is happening without drama or stories. Just be present, right now and right here. Let the past go. Stop worrying about tomorrow. Just for today, have a peaceful rest in the present moment. When a thought of the past or future arises, simply acknowledge it and let it pass like a cloud in the sky. Come back to what is happening, here and now. Just for today, let go of all your stories and live as a child in each moment.

Take a breathing break

Return to life with a positive affirmation

I am a diamond being polished into my brightest shining self

Photo: Michael Smith

Practice Session #30: Touch

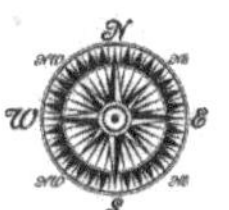

Reading and Contemplation

We all need to be touched. Unfortunately, our society has many beliefs and taboos about healthy touching that make these needs challenging. From time to time, there may be health limitations to being close to others. When we lose a loving relationship, it becomes even more difficult.

In recent years scientific research has identified the importance of physical touch in our lives. There are articles on the science of touch available by searching "touch" at https://greatergood.berkeley.edu/. It is particularly interesting to note that non-human primates spend ten to twenty percent of their waking time touching each other in grooming activities. Maybe we could learn something from those monkeys!

The latest research actually highlights how humans are wired to benefit from touch. Tiffany Field, a touch research expert, determined that preterm babies who received three 15-minute sessions of touch therapy each day for 5-10 days gained 47 percent more weight than premature babies receiving standard medical care. Touch benefits begin the moment we are born and continue all the days of our lives.

If there are no health deterrents, become a hugger! Learn to take the opportunity to hug people in appropriate settings. Make hugging a family ritual and take time to really hug versus the hello pat. Religious events are typically one of the safest community places to hug. If in doubt ask, "May I give you a hug?" Thich Naht Hahn, a zen monk, suggests mindful hugging. Hug the person heart to heart with your head on the left side of the person you are hugging. Gently place your hands on their back and avoid patting or hand movement. Become mindful and gently hug for three breath cycles. If you need to say anything make it a blessing.

If hugging is not an option, try some of the alternative techniques noted in the following action exercise.

Take a breathing break

Action exercise:

Even in times when hugging is not a healthy choice, there are options to meet your physical touch needs. Here are ideas on actions you can take today to increase touch in your life.

- Spend time petting or grooming your pet (adopt a cat or dog if you don't have one)
- Spend more time with the children in your life (kids naturally touch and hug)
- Take a long soaking bath and mindfully focus on washing and drying your body
- Learn to hug yourself
- Gently tap your breast bone (called the Thymus Tap — activating it boosts your immune system and meets touch needs)
- Learn Qigong tapping exercises (find a local training class or do an internet search, it is another easy self-care treatment)
- When appropriate, ask a family member or friend for a hug (remember they need to be touched as well)
- Schedule routine massages (find a discounted training facility if cost is a factor)
- Have a facial or other spa treatment (find a discount training facility if cost is a factor)
- Get a pedicure and/or manicure (find a discounted training facility if cost is a factor)

Become more conscious and mindful that touch is a normal human need. Schedule a massage, manicure, or pedicure, or schedule one a week for the next 4 weeks! Take actions to help your body. Make some time right now to try or find some of these services. Do that internet search on Qigong tapping and try one of the exercise programs available on YouTube. Go online and search spa, massage, nail services to schedule a treatment. Investigate discount services so you can schedule more touch activities for less money! Examples are training schools and Groupon if it is available locally.

Take a breathing break

Return to life with a positive affirmation

I take care of my body

Practice Session #31: Sleep

Reading and Contemplation

Sleep is our friend. Although it looks like we are doing nothing, our bodies are working very hard at night to keep us physically and mentally healthy. When we experience loss and grief sleep is sometimes elusive just when we need it most.

Loss of sleep upsets brain functions, including reasoning, problem solving, focus, and attention to detail. It also negatively impacts our mood, energy, and ability to focus. Lack of adequate sleep over time also increases our chance of developing depression.

During sleep our body actively restores the immune, nervous, skeletal and muscular systems. Adequate sleep also supports vital brain functions and helps us maintain mood and memory. Our body routinely heals itself and removes waste during sleep. The endocrine and immune systems rely on sleep to function normally. These are all body functions we want working for us during the stress of loss and grief.

We need adequate sleep to support healthy body functions. The National Institute of Health (at nia.nih.gov) recommends some basic steps to help you sleep better and avoid health problems related to sleep disturbance. Adults should aim for 7-9 hours of sleep each night. Babies need 16 hours per day, young children need 10 hours, and teenagers need 9 hours of sleep. Here are some tips that will help:

- Go to bed and wake up at the same time every day, even on weekends.
- Find ways to relax before bedtime each night.
- Avoid use of screens such as cell phones, computers, and televisions in your bedroom.
- Avoid meals, caffeine and alcohol late in the day.
- Exercise at regular times each day, but not within three hours of your bedtime.

- Avoid long naps (over 30 minutes) in the late afternoon or evening.
- Relaxation and deep-breathing techniques can significantly help with falling asleep.
- Search the internet for resources to support sleep. There are many tools like music, nature sounds and stories to help support sleep.
- Consult with your doctor before using over-the-counter sleep aids which may leave you feeling groggy in the morning and disrupt normal sleep functions.

Guard your sleep time. Give your body the sleep it needs to function correctly, and it will reward you! You deserve a good night's sleep every night.

Take a Breathing Break

Action exercise:

Go to YouTube and search sleep music and sleep relaxation. There are many free resources for sleeping better without medication. Bookmark the ones you like and try them over the next few weeks. They can be found in all faith and thought practices. Some work on physical relaxation, while others work on clearing the mind or generating peace. Try a variety to find which ones work best for you.

If you find meditation is helpful for falling asleep and sleeping well, you might evaluate meditation apps such as *Calm* and *Headspace*. Meditation may prove helpful in other areas of your life as well.

Take a Breathing Break

Return to life with a positive affirmation

I sleep well and awake renewed

Photo: Cheryl Muck

Practice Session #32: Unconditional Love

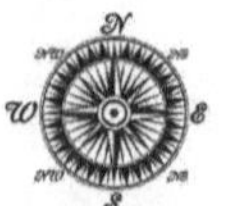

Reading and Contemplation

It is easy to feel left out or unfriended during grief. Typically, some friends simply cannot deal with loss or pain or grief. Some people are uncomfortable and unable to face death or personal crisis. They may avoid and possibly even abandon us at our darkest hour. If this happens, it is helpful to remember that their response has nothing to do with us. Their response really may have more to do with some old unresolved loss, hurt or pain. Some friends may avoid us because they feel uncomfortable and don't know what to say. Other friends may be there but provide too much advice or try to help by taking over. As time passes, some friends may seem to forget our recent loss. Others may think it is best not to bring it up, as if we have forgotten!

If we break a leg, our place of work understands that it will take at least 6 to 8 weeks to heal and possibly even longer to get back to normal. Have surgery and our doctor will give us a note for light duty when we return to work. Lose a loved one and work or school expects us back in 3 days, or maybe a week if our loss was close and unexpected.

Anyone may experience a loss that our culture does not acknowledge. These losses are especially difficult. Disenfranchised grief may include—loss of a pet, diagnosis of a sexually transmitted disease, loss of a body function, loss of a secret or unaccepted relationship, loss of a pregnancy, loss of someone to suicide, the list is unending. Unexpressed grief may lead to more intensified feelings including depression, powerlessness and anger. It may be especially helpful to get professional assistance in these instances.

When feeling battered down from grief, it can be beneficial to nurture unconditional love. We cannot control the response of others to our loss and grief, but we can control our response to them. We can consciously hold our friends and family in loving compassion. We can accept and love them regardless of their behavior. Most people are doing the best that they can in the circumstances. It may not be good enough, but it is still their best in the moment. The practice of loving-kindness helps strengthen, mend and heal relationships.

Unconditional love opens our hearts. It provides a window into another life. It allows us to see another's world without judgement or bias. We can love unconditionally—even those we do not agree with, even those that have done us harm, and even those that cannot love others unconditionally. We may not believe the same or hold the same values as another; regardless, we can love them. We accept their differences as a deeper understanding of what it means to be human.

Take a breathing break

Action exercise:

There are many loving-kindness meditations available on the internet or YouTube. Simply search loving-kindness meditation or Metta meditation.

Go online and select a loving-kindness meditation to do today. This meditation, done routinely can change your life. It generates a powerful sense of love and kindness and hope for society. It changes the way you see yourself and your fellow humans.

More than any other time, loss and grief remind us of our common humanity and our common pain. We are all wounded by life and in need of loving-kindness from ourselves, our loved ones, our friends and, yes, even strangers and enemies. Be an ambassador for loving-kindness. When you help another, you also help yourself.

Take a breathing break

Return to life with a positive affirmation

I love without condition

Photo: Michael Smith

Practice Session #33: Sorrow and Happiness

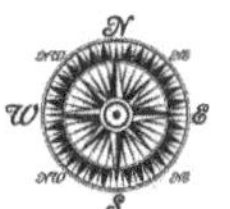

Reading and Contemplation

Life is full of both sorrow and happiness—some days one, some days the other and many days both. When grieving our tendency is to try to find a place where suffering no longer exists. We want to experience happiness again in our lives. But we finally discover they are flip sides of the same coin, and we cannot have one without the other. Both are different aspects of loving and caring.

Our lives are tangled up in a mind body connection that is sometimes difficult to understand. Sorrow or any other strong emotion is linked to both our mind and body. Physical bodies have chemicals and neurotransmitters involved in creating and sustaining all feelings, including sorrow. These chemicals and neurotransmissions are short lived and will naturally arise and pass away on their own. For sorrow to continue more than a few minutes, the thoughts that generated the sorrow must be recreated. Feelings only stay when we hold onto the thoughts that regenerate the chemicals which created them. If we focus on our loss and create stories about how bad it is or how it will never end, the body continues to generate the neurotransmissions that create the waves of sorrow. This is one of the reasons that sorrow seems to come and go in waves. When experiencing a wave of grief, try stopping and focusing on the breath. Mindfully breathe in and breathe out until the wave of painful sorrow passes. Tell your sorrow, "I am here for you right now. I will feel you and I will let you pass through me." Allow it to be and allow it to pass through and disperse. Remember the physical neurotransmitters creating that feeling are strong but very short lived.

If we fully experience life in each moment then we increase our happiness. But we will also experience our sorrow. If we choose to be present with the sorrow, it can naturally flow through us and dissipate. Being present and fully alive in both sorrow and happiness can bring insight and wisdom.

"When we learn to acknowledge, embrace, and understand our suffering, we suffer less. Not only that, but we're also able to go further and transform our suffering into understanding, compassion, and joy for ourselves and for others … the art of happiness is also and at the same time the art of knowing how to suffer well."

-Thich Nhat Hanh. No Mud, No Lotus

Take a breathing break

Action exercise:

Once you feel relaxed and quiet, center your breath on your heart area, focus as if you are breathing through your heart. Allow your heart to feel like it is growing with each breath cycle. Notice how big your heart feels. Focus on the big heart that goes beyond physical form. Focus on that unnamable reality you can feel in your heart area. Fully experience how immeasurable that part of your heart is. You are as vast as the sky, deep as the ocean, light as a cloud, wise as an ancient scholar and innocent as a newborn. Your big heart can hold eternity and all that is.

Your heart, or soul, or consciousness, or quiet center (whatever you call it) holds all of who you are with total acceptance and love. Your big heart can hold all your sorrow, your love, your joy, your faults, your memories, your anger, your best, your worst, all that you feel and all that you are beyond your body. There is room for all of it. There is room for a lifetime of love and joy and memories to survive.

Allow yourself to rest and relax into that vastness. All is well and all is calm in the quiet center of your being.

Take a breathing break

Return to life with a positive affirmation

I allow sorrow
but I water and tend
the seeds of happiness

Practice Session #34: Laughter

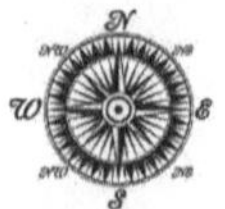

Reading and Contemplation

We all benefit from laughter. Yet, just when we need it most it is hard to find the healing lightness and sheer joy of laughter. During loss and grief, it is important to stay in touch with our own sense of humor. It is OK to laugh especially with family and friends. Shared laughter is a bonding experience that strengthens current relationships and forges new ones. Today notice the opportunities to laugh; and then just do it! Allow yourself the personal connection of laughter.

Research reveals that relationships and physical health are improved with full belly laughing. We know that endorphins and serotonin hormones are released when we laugh. These hormones make us feel good, decrease pain, and have an antidepressant effect. Our level of cortisol, the stress hormone, decreases when we laugh. Laughter also has an anti-inflammatory effect on our blood vessels and heart muscles, thus protecting and healing a broken heart! Laughter and a positive attitude also protect us from chronic diseases and even help lower the risk of heart attack and stroke. A good belly laugh activates your body's immune system (T cells) while also toning your belly muscles. Laughter is highly contagious and creates feelings of safety and togetherness. Overall, the research indicates that we should strive for at least 15 minutes of laughter a day.

How long has it been since you had a full belly laugh? Laughter is healing even when experiencing loss and grief. Smack that grief in the face with a laughter pie. There is always room for laughter, the spirit cleanser. Try it!

Take a Breathing Break

Action exercise:

Take time right now to DO SOMETHING THAT MAKES YOU LAUGH. Here are some ideas to get you started:

- YouTube search anything that is funny to you (I love "baby laughing")
- Watch a favorite sitcom
- Schedule a night out to see live comedy with a friend
- Make crazy faces with a child
- Tell funny stories about your lost loved one
- Watch an old LUCY show

Take a breathing break

Return to life with a positive affirmation

I welcome my sense of humor

Practice Session #35: Fear

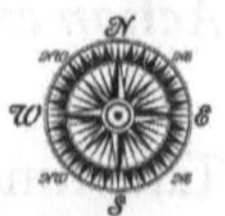

Reading and Contemplation

Fear is natural when we encounter any significant loss. We fear being alone. We are afraid we will never love another or that another will never love us. We fear the pain of living with our loss. We fear that others will treat us differently. We fear we will never feel whole again. The list goes on.

Fear arises with any loss perceived as a threat. When we experience fear, our physical bodies respond to the danger with a fight or flight response. When danger is perceived the body releases hormones. Those hormones slow down body functions not needed for survival and sharpen body functions which might help us survive. The heart races, breathing quickens, and muscles tense.

A death or other loss is typically perceived as a threat and the natural physiological functions kick in automatically. These physical responses memorializing the event in our brain. Therefore, our memories of the loss event may be fragmented, but they are usually durable and include senses and details such as sights, sounds, odors, time of day, colors, etc. Fears may be triggered in the future when similar events arise. For example, when we visit a hospital our brain may unconsciously classify and predict a danger or threat.

When fear arises, stop, breathe deeply and slowly. Greet your fear with respect and thank it for bringing needed energy to your body. "Hello fear, I know you are there, thank you for taking care of me and for bringing me needed energy. I am OK, you can trust me to get through this."

Acknowledge and allow fear without letting it take control of your life. Stay present in the moment, painful as it may be. Breathe, and go to the calm center of your being and focus on the breath. Fighting fear only strengthens it. Use the energy of fear to see the world clearly and to take new actions. Change your attitude about fear. New possibilities arise when we learn to identify the energy of fear and focus it on our breath. Take a few minutes to calm the body. Once the parasympathetic nervous system is engaged, the fear gradually dissipates and thoughts become clearer.

Take a breathing break

Action exercise:

Contemplate on the role of fear in your life. Take time to journal or just spend time thinking about the following:

- When was the first time you ever felt fear?
- What is the most common cause of fear in your life?
- What have you done to overcome fear in the past?

Contemplate on how another's fear impacts your relationship with them. Take time to journal or just spend time thinking about the following:

- When have you identified fear in another?
- Do you feel fearful when another exhibits fear?
- How can you acknowledge and help another with their fear?

Contemplate on how to change your relationship with fear. Take time to journal or just spend time thinking about the following:

- How does fear usually manifest in your body and mind?
- Do you feel it in your throat, your gut, your neck?
- Identify the symptoms you have when fear is present.
- Make a plan on how to respond to those symptoms and your fear when it next arises.

Take a breathing break

I use the energy of fear
to return focus to the breath

Practice Session #36: Anger

Reading and Contemplation

You will get angry about your loss. It is OK. It is normal. It is right. We all experience anger. Allow it to be. You have been hurt. Life is not always fair, and you have no control over what happens. Anger is a response to fear, hurt, and sadness. It is a self-defense mechanism trying to stop a perceived threat. The body responds by releasing adrenalin and noradrenalin, the heart rate increases and blood pressure elevates. In such a physical state, it is easy to lose all perspective.

It may help to become the watcher when anger arises. Simply observe your anger. Watch your anger as if watching a toddler try to open a locked cabinet. Watch with love and understanding and maybe even humor in your heart. Watch the building frustration, the desire, the hostility toward the cabinet which separates him from what he wants. Watch the child learn that everything she wants will not be given.

Allow the struggle, allow the learning. When the anger and frustration and hostility lessen, hold yourself (like that toddler) in love and understanding. Send love and acceptance and healing to yourself. You deserve to be happy and free from the pain of anger.

As you safely release your anger, try not to get too caught up in it. Let it arise, experience it, and let it go. Balance is key. Experience the anger but do not allow it to take over. Remember that spending too much time with anger does not serve your highest interest. We move closer to peace and acceptance when we acknowledge and transform anger. Allowing anger to flow and pass on leaves room for more positive emotions to arise.

Take a breathing break

Consider using the Breathing practice: "Breathing and Visualizing Light Practice" on page 34 or my You Tube channel.

Action exercise:

Today, right now, give yourself a healing gift. Allow anger to be, then release it. It is better to identify and acknowledge your anger early and safely release it. Take some time right now to identify and release anger in healthy non-destructive ways. This exercise may help you avoid the overwhelming experience of repressed anger which can arise full blown when least expected and in the worst time and place.

Just in case you are wondering, it is natural to be angry with who or what you have lost! And it is also alright to be angry with a higher power - God, Spirit, the Universe. One of my favorite Hospice chaplains used to say, "It's OK to be angry with God - she's big enough to take it!" That always makes me smile.

There are healthy ways to acknowledge and release anger. Take time right now to do whatever works for you, as long as it is not destructive to you or another.

- Hit a pillow or find a punching bag,
- Park in a remote area - scream and yell in your car (the screaming chamber),
- Beat a drum or pot/pan,
- Write a nasty letter and burn it in a ceremony.

Take a breathing break

Return to life with a positive affirmation

I acknowledge my loss and release the related anger

Practice Session #37: Sadness

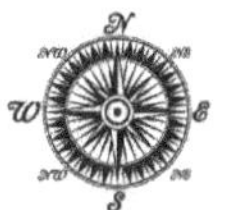

Reading and Contemplation

Profound sadness is expected with loss and grief. Sadness is a natural human reaction to loss and grief. Like all emotions, sadness is temporary. Sadness comes into your awareness, grows and then dissipates; it comes and goes as all emotions do. Try to keep sadness from moving in and becoming a roommate. Sometimes, sadness can become a frequent companion and totally overwhelm us. We all suffer from change, loss, separation, and death. We all know this, and yet we distance ourselves from this truth. We want life to be different than it is. We want the upside of joy and love but not the downside of change and loss.

Sprinkled in amongst the sadness, there will also be moments of comfort, laughter, and even peace. When those feelings arise take them in and allow them to grow. It may feel unfaithful to our lost love, but it is not. Someday, hopefully soon, their memory will include their eternal desire for our happiness.

As we learn to live consciously and be mindful, life becomes better. Life can once again be full of meaning and joy and even love. It is a choice we make every day. We decide to do the hard work of grieving. We decide to go on. We decide to honor life and our lost love. We decide to be present with the truth of our reality. We decide to genuinely live. We decide to turn darkness into light.

Breathe deeply and embrace your strength. Make the choice to bless yourself with a full life. Here and Now.

Take a breathing break

Action exercise:

There are actions we can take to help us deal with the normal sadness of loss and grief. Try some or all of the list below. Pick one out and take time to do it right now! Better yet, create some specific joyful actions of your own!

Schedule at least one activity you truly enjoy every day - put it on your calendar as a reminder. Schedule activities. Don't wait for joy to happen, invite it into your life.

- Connect with other people. Here are some ways to do that — make a call to a friend or family member, talk to your spiritual advisor, take a class with complete strangers and allow yourself to become someone new.
- Watch funny TV shows, movies, YouTube, or old comedies. There is healing in laughter.
- Spend time with a loved pet. Walk outside and breath in nature. Go to a concert and get lost in the music. Go to an art museum. Do anything that brings you joy and insight.
- Move your body. Your body naturally releases happy endorphins when you exercise!
- Eat healthy. Take a healthy cooking class or join a dinner group.
- Avoid self-medicating with alcohol or drugs; they distort your perspective and delay your healing.
- Schedule a bedtime and keep it. We need at least 8 to 9 hours of sleep a night, especially when our bodies are healing. Set a bedtime notice on your phone.
- SIMPLIFY your life. Living simply has its own beauty and joy. Take this time to experience a simpler and more meaningful life.

You may find that some of these activities change your life! Consciously making choices to improve your life is empowering. You are on the road to fulfilling your destiny. Be all you can be. Live strong, smart and happy.

Take a breathing break

Return to life with a positive affirmation

I embrace my sadness with compassion

Photo: Cheryl Muck

Practice Session #38: Depression

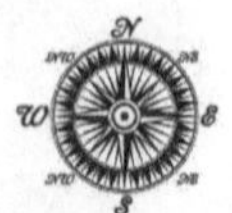

Reading and Contemplation

The sadness of grief comes and goes and is normal. Most of us have periods of sadness in response to life's struggles and losses. Obviously, sadness is expected as a normal response to loss and grief. It is important to be present with grief as you adapt to a changed reality, adjust to life without the loved one and recover a new balanced life. Burying your feelings and loss with unneeded medication is not helpful. However, when the normal grief process becomes complicated and ongoing, then medication and therapy may help get us back on track.

When feelings related to grief become overwhelming, last for long periods of time, cause health or physical changes, or keep you from living an active normal life, a physician can help you determine if your grief has triggered clinical depression. Clinical depression is not the same as the sadness of grief. Doctors can evaluate your symptoms for clinical depression or recommend a mental health specialist for diagnosis. Recognizing the symptoms to discuss with your health care advisor is very helpful. Here are some of the common symptoms of clinical depression:

- Mental focus challenges (inability to concentrate or remember details).
- Inability to make decisions or take actions on plans.
- Physical or mental fatigue.
- Feeling unworthy, guilty or helpless.
- Persistent sadness, anxiety or loneliness (anxiety and depression are common together).
- Believing everything is hopeless (including thoughts/attempts at suicide).
- Increased irritability.
- Changes in sleep patterns (excessive wakefulness or sleeping too much).

- Restlessness and inability to relax.
- Loss of interest in previously enjoyed activities (hobbies, activities, sex, etc.).
- Appetite changes (overeating or loss of appetite).
- Physical symptoms or issues that do not resolve (pain, headaches, digestion issues, etc.).

Depression can take over and impair every aspect of life—work, play, relationships, and even rest. It can take the joy out of everything. If you think you have depression, seek help. Talk to your doctor if you feel that would be helpful. Taking action to get help will probably be challenging, as the inability to take action is a common symptom of depression. Seek the help of a friend if necessary. Sometimes a friend or loved one can help you select and go to a therapist. Do whatever it takes to break the cycle of depression and get your life back. Medical treatment for depression includes medication and mental health therapy.

Take a breathing break

Action exercise:

Review the list of depression symptoms and identify any areas of concern. Contemplate your feelings and coping skills. Ask yourself some hard questions. Here are some questions to consider:

- Does it seem that I am generally moving forward on the path to recover?
- Do I feel like I am growing stronger and adapting to my new reality?
- Do I have hope for the future?
- Am I taking care of myself? Am I getting enough rest, eating healthy, interacting with friends/family and getting back to my routines?
- Do I have persistent health issues that arose after my loss? Do I have issues related to sleep or appetite?

- Do I feel mentally strong? Am I having unusual fatigue (physical or mental)? Difficulty making decisions? Inability to concentrate, make decisions or take actions?

If you have a safe, honest and loving friend or family member, consider talking to them about how they feel you are coping. Discuss your progress through the grief process. Talk openly and verify the accuracy of your self-perceptions. Sometimes another viewpoint can help clarify our progress and mental states. If you or your friend think you may have an issue with depression, contact your physician or a mental health professional for individualized care.

Take a breathing break

Return to life with a positive affirmation

I take good care of myself and seek assistance when appropriate

Practice Session #39: Learning from Difficult Days

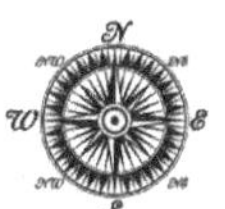

Reading and Contemplation

When life is at its worst, it is very hard to be at our best. Most of us loose our sense of balance. Nothing in the world seems just and fair. Joy disappears. Hope for the future abandons us. Sometimes, we even get sucked into the bottomless pit of depression.

Railing and pushing back against the reality of what has happened rarely improves anything. There is not a fix to every problem. In such times, we have to accept reality as broken and imperfect. Broken things allow the light in, so we can look for that light. We can focus on getting through to the next day and the next and the next. One of those days a new light will dawn.

We can mindfully set the intention to be our best self regardless of our worst experiences. Here are some behaviors or practices that help most of us do that.

Calm the body. You can focus on the breath to calm your physical body. You can calmly walk or move the body to stay present in this difficult moment. Physical activity helps ground us in the present moment and decreases our anxiety.

Calm the mind. Use whatever works for you — prayer, breathing, a mantra, etc. Use your mental chatterbox in positive ways by using statements like, this is the way things are right now. I have the strength to deal with right now. Tomorrow I will deal with tomorrow.

Connect with spirit, soul, life force, God, or whatever you call that universal truth that we experience. How we touch spiritual truth varies and does not matter. What matters is that we draw on the endless love and strength that abides in our sacred space. Go to that place of abiding quiet, peace and love. Go there for rest and healing.

After significant loss and grief, our world is different. Change happens every day, but the changes related to loss and grief are always significant. In some ways, we will probably be stronger and better. In some ways, we may be more fragile and vulnerable. Life constantly changes us with or without loss and grief. It is the most consistent reality for everyone. If we consciously make an effort to stay aware and mindful of our reality, we typically grow and learn from life. We can become better and wiser and kinder as a result of adversity.

Take a breathing break

Action exercise:

Loss and grief have taught me to be kinder and gentler with myself and others. When out in the world, we continually encounter folks that are hurt and afraid and angry. We usually know who they are because of their bad behavior. After my experiences with loss and grief, I see those situations differently. I remember a day at Houston. I was at M.D. Anderson with my parents so my father could receive lymphoma treatment. I felt responsible for everything going right - even my Dad getting cured of lymphoma. Dad needed something from the store, I don't even remember what it was. I had less than an hour to run and pick it up before our next appointment. The entire trip to the store was a nightmare because of my stress. I was inconsiderate to other drivers. I was snippy with the service staff helping me find things. I was so upset by the time I checked out that I was rude and tears were streaming down my face.

For some reason, I managed to watch the entire event while knowing I was out of control but unable to be or do anything different. What a bad memory. And luckily it comes back whenever I run into someone out of control for no apparent reason. I lightly smile and think, "yep we can all lose control when life gets too painful." Now, after my initial reaction to a bad encounter, I stop and try to imagine why the offender is acting unpleasant. I try to walk in their shoes and look through their eyes. When I cannot identify a reason for their bad behavior, I assume that they are in physical or emotional pain. I then take a moment to slowly breathe three times while consciously sending them loving-kindness and compassion. When it is possible, I also try to give them a kindness that they can see or feel. Maybe I give them a smile, a joke to lighten the mood, a helping hand, an offer for them to have my place in line, a kind word. I send them some small kindness that might make their day just a little brighter.

Today, look at everyone you meet with kindness, compassion, and love. Smile and genuinely hope the best for them. When someone is unkind, immediately think, "WOW, they need extra good things to happen to them today." Send them double the kindness, compassion and love. Take action to be a bright shining light in their day!

Take a breathing break

Return to life with a positive affirmation

I am kind to everyone knowing that today they may be in pain

Practice Session #40: Loneliness

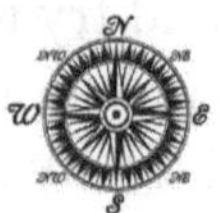

Reading and Contemplation

We are social beings. We are designed and are then taught to live in community, so both nature and nurture make us social animals. We spend much of our lives seeking meaningful physical and emotional connections. Most of us find comfort and support and completion in our relationships. Loving human connections and experiences make us feel better about ourselves and the world we live in.

When a loved one is in pain or sick or injured, we may try anything to help them. Nothing seems too much or too far when we are trying to hold on to someone we love. We promise anything or go anywhere or encourage any experimental medical treatment. We hold on tightly unwilling to let someone go when they are ready and want to depart. We do not want to be left alone.

Our life seems to radically change when someone we care about dies, or leaves us, or emotionally disconnects. The loss can feel like a reality shift which leaves us off balance and out of focus. The feeling of loneliness may seem more than we can bear. Sometimes, we try to avoid loneliness by filling our lives with people and activities and responsibilities. At other times, we may decide to embrace our humanity and experience our loneliness.

It is normal to feel lonely from time to time. We can feel lonely in a crowd or even with a loved one. Loneliness is part of our human nature. There is much to be learned from loneliness. It teaches us that each person, each moment, each relationship is precious.

Each relationship deserves to be honored and cherished for what it is or what it was. We are less likely to sabotage future relationships if we stay present and experience the loss. We will never have another relationship that replaces the one lost. And yet, if we allow ourselves to take a chance, other relationships will support and nourish and heal our hearts. Life can go on. We can survive loneliness even though some days that is hard to believe.

Periods of loneliness come and go throughout our life. Loneliness can easily invade our heart when we feel isolated and disconnected. Yet, at the core of our being there is always a wholeness. You may call it the sacred center, the heart, the spirit, God. Even when we do not feel it, the wholeness of the sacred center is there lovingly waiting for us. When we relax and quiet our busy mind, we can experience the sacred center where loneliness dissolves. We can experience that love where we are all ONE, connected and filled with peace, joy and love.

Take a breathing break

Action exercise:

Give yourself permission to

FEEL YOUR LOSS
Have a good cry
Punch a pillow
Scream in a safe place
Mourn the loss of connection

Give yourself permission to

CONSIDER HUMAN NATURE
Our bodies are temporary
Our minds evolve and change
Our atoms reconfigure
Our energy is eternal

Give yourself permission to

CONSIDER HUMAN CONNECTION

The joy of connection
The comfort of loving touch
Shared memories of the past
Mutual anticipation of the future

Give yourself permission to

CONSIDER LOVE'S BENEFITS
Feel the pleasure of remembering love
Feel the comfort of being loved
Feel the embrace of timeless love
Feel the joy of eternal love

Take a breathing break

Return to life with a positive affirmation

Loneliness resolves when
I experience my connection to all that is

Photo: Michael Smith

Practice Session #41: Limits

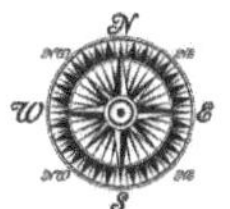

Reading and Contemplation

Sometimes our grief can wear us down. Yet at the same time, grief can uncover unknown depths of spirit. Loss can teach us difficult but important life lessons. When we stay mindful of our feelings and the feelings of those around us, we open our hearts to experience the intensity of life even in the midst of loss or death.

At times mindfulness comes naturally when we are in grief. When we experience loss our senses are heightened, our emotions are more intense, and our bonds are strengthened. Allow that intensity to arise since it supports us and generates healing. Occasionally, there can even be a poignant joy to being fully alive, vibrant and aware in the midst of loss or death.

At other times, grief can overwhelm and overcome our balance. We can become stuck in our sorrow which decreases the ability to heal. Healing requires movement and flow. If we feel stuck, it may be helpful to observe our grief and determine how we are responding to the changes in our life. When needed, set limits. Here are some examples:

- Anger is OK and should be allowed; hurting ourselves or others is not helpful.
- Guilt is normal and expected; turning it into a sense of unworthiness is not helpful.
- Acceptance is a good thing; using it to avoid dealing with the hard stuff is not helpful.
- A private pity party can restore; making the pity party into a way of life is not helpful.

Create balance by setting limits that allow emotions to flow and healing to occur. Emotions arise, are experienced, and move on; that is their nature.

When we hang on to the past or to any one emotion, we can create a self-absorbed stagnation. Avoid stagnation by flowing with the moments' emotions.

It is your life, and you can do this! You have control even when grief sometimes makes you think you don't.

Take a breathing break

Action exercise:

Sit quietly and be with your feelings. Observe your emotions. Be with each feeling as you experience it. Every feeling has a right to be heard and experienced. Each emotion has something to teach you about what is going on in your mind. Emotions are not permanent or solid but rather internal energy you produce. Once you acknowledge and accept negative feelings, they typically move on and shift to a higher feeling energy.

Take time to experience the tears and sorrow. Be present with your pain, and allow yourself to experience it. Feel crocodile tears roll down your face, feel the jaggedness of your breath, and feel the release of pain. Feel the sorrow gradually abate and settle and ease. Wash your face and feel the coolness of the water against skin. Notice that you automatically know how to take care of yourself in this moment.

Our emotional suffering is tied to wanting reality to be other than what it is. Acknowledging an emotion is usually the first step toward accepting and releasing the pain of life. Once acknowledged, it is typically easier to let a negative feeling flow into the past.

We are in control; even when we allow ourselves to feel out of control. We create our own world and life. We are free to choose our own path. We move through our fear of being alone, knowing that being alone does not mean we are lonely. We take action in spite of anxiety, learning that we are stronger than we think. When we successfully weather a crisis, we become more independent, stronger, different and even happier.

Take a breathing break

Return to life with a positive affirmation

I am growing and improving every day

Photo: Cheryl Muck

Practice Session #42: Suffering

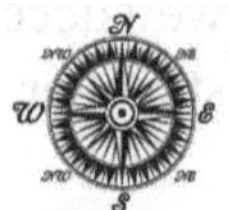

Reading and Contemplation

Suffering is tied to our inability to accept what is right here and right now. We want things to be other than what they are. This is the root cause of suffering. We grasp at memories of the past or visions of the future. This makes it impossible to be present and at peace with the glory of the present moment, even in all its imperfection.

No matter how hard we try to deny it, loss and grief are normal and unavoidable realities of life. Sometimes our loss, grief, and suffering can over-balance the abundance, wonder, and happiness of life. There is great freedom in accepting and embracing both. I love the way Joseph Campbell says it:

"The first step to the knowledge of the wonder and mystery of life is the recognition of the monstrous nature of the earthly human realm as well as its glory."

When it comes to grief, accepting and walking through our pain and suffering can bring dignity and much personal growth. We can gently hold our grief as we honor our painful loss. We can consciously be with the loss. Holding our loss with dignity and respect is healthy. Suppressing or repressing our natural feelings may cause a longer recovery.

When we grieve and are present with the pain, we learn that our heart is big enough to hold the pain, endure the loss, and ultimately grow. We can consciously choose to witness our grief, anger, fear, and pain and allow life to be what it is. Grasping at what was or could have been creates more pain. We open ourselves to growth and acceptance when we gently show ourselves compassion and acknowledge reality as it is.

We can observe and honor our loss without judgement, accepting it as part of the monstrous nature of being alive. We can feel the hurt without generating a negative storyline about it. Our choices can allow grief to come and go, passing like a dark cloud in the sky. Create a way to grieve that will honor your suffering and lead you to appreciate the wonder and mystery of life. Discover a way to live with joy beyond your grief.

Take a breathing break

Action exercise:

Set the alarm for ten minutes. Once you are relaxed and focused from your breath practice, focus on your beating heart. If it helps, place your hand on your heart or find and follow your pulse. Feel the strength of the heart as it pumps nourishment to every cell of the body. Feel the oxygen penetrating each cell with life. Focus on the heart and the blood pumping throughout the body. Feel the body receiving nourishment and energy. Note how all this happens naturally and continually without any conscious effort. Rejoice in how the body knows how to take care of itself. Continue until you feel full of life and energy.

Continue focusing on the breath and the life energy surging through the body until the alarm calls you back. Gently return to life with an open heart and an acceptance for life just as it is. Carry energy and peace with you today.

Take a breathing break

Return to life with a positive affirmation

I acknowledge and honor my grief

Practice Session #43: Self-denial

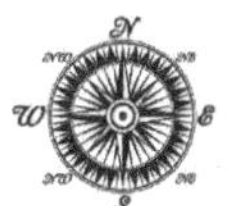

Reading and Contemplation

When we respond to loss with stoic behavior, we deny and ignore the natural feelings associated with loss. In American culture, many endure pain and hardship without complaint, believing this is a virtue. The predominant belief is that feelings should be controlled and certainly not displayed in public. This is a form of misplaced self-denial. No one wins when someone dishonestly denies normal and natural feelings related to loss.

The Christian culture values selflessness and sacrifice for the good of others. This belief has value in many instances. However, it can create complications when it gets tangled up with loss and grief. Stoic behavior related to significant loss requires repression of feelings - this is not a selfless act. Self-denial in response to loss serves no one; we can hardly be of service to others and our community if we do not heal our own losses and grief. We cannot give compassion if we do not already possess it.

The only way out of grief is to go through it. We and everyone around us will continue to suffer if we do not deal with our loss and grief when it occurs. Through the years, unresolved grief returns and damages our relationships and our happiness.

Be present. Be honest. Be with your feelings. Be strong enough to deal with your loss in the here and now. Be in this moment, hard as it is. That is the true measure of your strength.

Take a breathing break

Action exercise:

Today, take care of yourself by honoring your feelings. Spend a few minutes thinking about how you honestly feel. Release all expectations and thoughts about how you should expect to feel. Your true feelings deserve to be honored. Honor them by writing them down. If you want to release and let those feelings go, hold a burning ceremony. Find a safe place to burn the written notes about your honest feelings. Remember, recovery is a process. Deal with your feelings in the moment, one day at a time. There is healing in experiencing and processing your feelings now and letting them go! Tomorrow is a new day, and you may have new feelings with which to deal. Don't leave today's feelings to muddy up tomorrow.

How to create a burning ceremony:

- Light a candle with reverence and love in your heart.
- Contemplate your loss. Write down the most honest feelings about your loss. Pour out your heart. Say everything you haven't been able to say aloud. Write until you are done.
- Take the paper to a safe place to burn. (Use a sink, fireplace, bowl, fire pit, etc. Use good judgement; you know what is safe and perfect for your needs.)
- Fold the paper over. On the outside write: "I am ready to release these feelings. With gratitude for what was and with love and compassion for all involved, I release these feelings. I release these feelings for me. I release these feelings for my loss. I release these feelings for all those remaining. I release these feelings so all may be free of suffering."
- Hold the paper to your lips; kiss and blow out on the paper three times. Each time you blow focus your intention on lovingly releasing the past.
- Place the paper in a safe place and light it on fire. Watch those old feelings burn. As they burn visualize them leaving room in your heart for new feelings and a healthy new start, like a forest fire prepares the land for new growth.
- At the end of the burning, ask for renewing energy to enter your life. Do this through prayer or a positive affirmation or whatever has meaning for you.

Sometimes, it helps to have a non-judgmental conversation about our honest feelings. If this is something that may help you, find a person you trust completely and tell them you need to have a safe conversation with them about your feelings. Tell the truth based on today's contemplation. Be honest about your feelings and what you are going through.

Take it all in
Anger
Fear
Hate
Love
Helplessness
Denial
Hope
Confusion
Sadness
Guilt
Acceptance

Take it in
Be with it
Let it move through
And allow it to pass on

Take a breathing break

Return to life with a positive affirmation

I deserve happiness

Practice Session #44: Becoming One

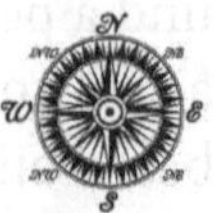

Reading and Contemplation

Sometimes, especially during times of stress, the mind can become closed and small and restricted. During those times one specific thought or feeling can overtake and overwhelm us. At other times, our mind feels open and free and spacious. During these times, no single thought or feeling totally takes over. Our mind and life feels safe as there is space enough for all that arises.

Most of us prefer times when we feel open, free, and spacious. Fortunately, there are specific actions we can take to help us feel that way. These practices help us resolve stress and ruminating thoughts by creating space in our mind and life.

How long has it been since you lay on the earth and looked up at the sky? Whatever the answer, isn't that too long? Remember the wonder of looking up into the never-ending sky or watching the clouds float by or sinking into the depths of a starry sky? We may become one with the stars and the ever-expanding universe, or we may shrink into our tiny self when face to face with the vastness of the universe. We may feel separate, small, unsubstantial and meaningless; or we may feel expansive, joyful, safe and one with all that is. Becoming One is about consciously choosing to feel connected, expansive and whole. I personally call that the Holy One. You may call it God or Buddha or Allah or Yahweh or the Universe, whatever word has meaning for you. The label has less meaning than the feeling of peace and wholeness and freedom.

Mindfulness and meditation practices can help us create more space to reach an open and peaceful state. Prayer can also help to reach that state when the focus is on resting in God's never-ending love and grace. Any spiritual practice that serves to expand us beyond ourselves helps us feel our oneness with all that is.

The following action exercise is a powerful healing meditation/

prayer. It will help you create a safe holy space to be present with your loss and grief. Once this practice is learned, you can escape and rest here anytime you are feeling boxed in, limited, stressed out or alone. This space can become your safe haven or heaven, a place to go and see the bigger picture, identify possibilities and find more informed solutions to life's problems. When you take actions to create an open and spacious mind, your life becomes increasingly calm, free and joyful.

Take a breathing break

Action exercise:

Try the meditation/prayer below. See if it helps you create space in your heart and mind.

- Sit comfortably and close your eyes.
- Imagine being surrounded by an infinite, perfectly clear, blue sky.
- Rest your mind on this infinite sky. Feel the spaciousness and freedom of floating in this safe blue sky.
- Now visualize a small light in your heart. Focus on that light.
- With each breath, gradually expand that light until it completely surrounds you. No walls, no boundaries, nothing confining you.
- With each breath, gradually expand that light into the clear blue sky and beyond into infinity.
- When you lose focus and thoughts enter your mind, simply acknowledge them and return to that light glowing in your heart. Gently return and breath by breath continue to expand that light until it reaches all that is.
- Appreciate the beauty of that space you have created. Appreciate its spaciousness and openness. Feel the total freedom of limitless space and time. Feel the presence of all that is. Know that this space includes all that has ever been and all that will ever be.

- Allow this space and light to permeate all that you are. Feel the spaciousness of your body and mind and soul. Although there is much openness and emptiness, paradoxically this space includes all that is, all that was and all that will ever be. Do not get lost in emptiness but rather be present with the fullness and freedom of all that is.

Rest in this feeling. Allow yourself to feel complete and connected with the Holy One or God or Buddha or Allah or Yahweh or the Universe. Use any name you choose to call that undefinable experience of ONENESS.

When you feel safe and free and rested, gently and gradually bring yourself back to the current time and place.

Take a breathing break

Return to life with a positive affirmation

I feel safe and loved and free
in BIG SKY

Photo: Cheryl Muck

Practice Session #45: Gratitude

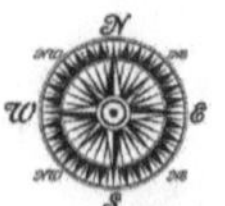

Reading and Contemplation

Gratitude is a state of mind. It has very little to do with reality and everything to do with how we react to reality. I think we all know this to be true. We have witnessed someone full of gratitude for what little they have. We have known people with more than they need who never show thankfulness.

Loss and grief can rob us of our gratitude. When we have lost much it is easy to lose sight of what we still have. An aching heart does not naturally fill with gratitude. It may require practice to appreciate what we still have.

It is worth the effort to practice gratitude. Psychologists find that feeling grateful actually boosts happiness over time. Brain scans show that participants actively experiencing and expressing gratitude develop prefrontal cortex changes. These changes increase future experiences of gratitude. Consciously counting your blessings actually changes your brain! Psychologists know that practicing gratitude increases happiness and supports both physical and psychological health. Research shows that people who are grateful experience less pain, insomnia, mental health issues and depression. Grateful people have stronger immune systems, relationships and resiliency.

Take a breathing break

Action exercise:

We can all increase our gratitude. All we have to do is routinely practice gratitude. Throughout your day notice big and small joys. Rejoice in gratitude for those joys. Try to establish the practice of noticing when good things happen and take a moment to smile and feel grateful.

Right now, take out a pen and paper and write down three things for which you are grateful. They can be big or small issues; all gratitude counts! Consider making a habit of writing three gratitude statements a day until gratitude becomes a habit. Keep a little notepad to keep with you to note gratitude when it occurs.

If you are grateful for someone in your life, write them a card and let them know how grateful you are that they are in your life. Not only will your heart fill with gratitude but the person who receives the note will have a moment of joy and gratitude as well.

Take a breathing break

Return to life with a positive affirmation

I practice gratitude every day

Practice Session #46: Love

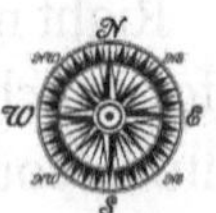

Reading and Contemplation

The great religions, masters, philosophers, prophets and sages agree that love is essential to a life well lived. When we experience a loss, surrendering to the healing process is the most loving thing we can do for ourselves. Healing is natural; it will happen if we allow it.

Our ability to love others is directly tied to our ability to love ourselves. Accept yourself as you are, perfect even with all your imperfections. Strive to shine light on your best self while accepting all that you are. As long as no one else is harmed, allow yourself to be and do and enjoy anything that makes you feel good and whole and free. Learn what makes you happy and do the things you love. Nurture yourself. You are worthy of your own love. You are amazing and strong and deserve to be happy. When you fill yourself with love, love will naturally overflow to others.

Loving yourself is the best gift you can give yourself. Loving yourself is the best gift you can give your family. Loving yourself is the best gift you can give your neighbors. Loving yourself is the best gift you can give the world!

Love expands our world, our life and our joy. Fear contracts our world, our life and our joy. Living in love connects us to the Spirit larger than ourselves. Even difficult times become easier when we open our hearts to love.

Choose love over and over and over again. Even when it breaks your heart, love still abides. Love heals our heart and gives us strength to carry on. Allow love to heal your broken heart.

Take a breathing break

Action exercise:

Today open your heart and grieve wholeheartedly.
It takes love and courage to grieve well.
Bravely face the love lost.
Know your brokenness.
And also
remember joy,
remember love,
remember the one lost.

It is painful,
lovingly be with the pain anyway.
It is difficult,
lovingly embrace the difficulty anyway.
It is the natural cycle of life,
lovingly accept the cycle of life anyway.
It is easy to close the heart,
lovingly open the heart anyway.

May peace and joy abide
and follow you
all the days of your life!

Take a breathing break

Return to life with a positive affirmation

I open my heart to love

Photo: Cheryl Muck

MOVING FORWARD

Finishing this book is difficult; as it is difficult to let go of grief. It is hard to feel finished. I have spent nearly two years writing this, and it will never be perfect. However, as those of you who know me well understand, I could ramble on forever. But it is time to let this book out in the world to do what it was intended to do. I have been blessed by its writing. May it also bless you as you process your grief.

My hope is that you now have some tools to keep you moving forward. May they help you expand your skills in living your best life! You deserve to be happy. You deserve to have a good and full life. Your lost love would want you to be happy and have a wonderful life. Honor their loss by living a life filled with joy and an increased depth of appreciation.

There are many wonderful resources to help you on your path forward. Seek out those resources and utilize them. Allow me to leave you with one thought I routinely say: There is a world of difference between knowing the path and walking the path. Some days it is a mighty struggle to walk the path. Other days the path is wide and clear. So, go out and walk your path. Take actions to heal your heart. Be present with your grief and pain. When the pain and loss become too much, use your breath to calm your body.

Live fully present in each moment, releasing the past and allowing the future to unfold on its own. Plant and tend seeds for a joy-filled future, but don't try to open the blossom. Rather, allow it to unfold naturally on its own. Your life is a beautiful blossom. Trust that the universe is unfolding with love and hope for you.

Namaste, that which is holy in me greets that which is holy in you! We are all connected. May we each practice living and acting into that truth.

Photo: Cheryl Muck

ACKNOWLEDGEMENTS

Thank You
To All Who Have Supported
Me On The Path

Where this book misses the the mark,
the fault lies with me not them.

Book design and editing:
Rich and Patty McNeill
This book was published with their expert assistance; I could not have done it alone. I value both their friendship and wisdom.

Patty was my partner and editor extraordinaire. Her gentle guidance and patience are amazing. She encouraged me every step of the way. During the long journey, when necessary she kicked me in the pants to get with it and finish the book.

Rich did all the book assembly and design work. His creativity and technical skills are amazing. His time and dedication to this book are truly appreciated. Rich is an extraordinary artist which is evident in his layout of the book. Artwork at www.mcneillart.com

YouTube Presence:
Nico Nico
Nico did all the heavy lifting on developing and editing the accompanying YouTube channel materials. He is an old soul that graces my life with knowledge and wisdom. His support has been amazing and I will be forever indebted to him for his assistance.

Photography and reader:
Michael Smith
Michael graciously shared some of his beautiful photos for the book. The pictures he shared are noted throughout the book. His photography mentoring also impacted all of my pictures. It was a joy to collaborate with him on the visual impact of the book.

Hospice Readers and Supporters:

Gary Springer, an award-winning Hospice Nurse and dear friend, provided invaluable advice and suggestions that improved this book immensely. Watching him with Hospice patients and families is an amazing experience. His hospice work alone should earn him a star-filled crown in glory.

Celeste Roberson Smith and Jean Mason Davies, the first two Clinical Hospice Directors of the VNA of Dallas and my dear friends, both provided critical support and valuable input. They not only made this book better, they have made me a better person.

I cannot hope to name all the nurses, managers, physicians, chaplains, social workers, caregivers, loving family members and hospice patients that influenced this book. I count it a privilege to have been able to take a few steps with them on their extraordinary journeys. All that is good in this book belongs to them.

Readers influencing the format and content of the book:

Mark Davies, friend and avid reader, provided suggestions and support along the way.

Linda Moore, a dear friend and mother grieving the loss of her son, provided helpful support, encouragement and insights.

Beatrice Green was there commenting, suggesting and encouraging me to keep moving and get it done.

Mindfulness practitioners:

Cornell Kinderknecht, Co-Director Dallas Meditation Center and fellow Kansan, is a steady influence and mentor in my mindfulness practice. His friendship and support have kept me focused on the mindfulness path since 2013. Cornell's music is an inspiration! Check it out at: www.Cornellk.com

The Mindful Monday participants at the Dallas Meditation Center teach me something new about walking the path of mindfulness every Monday!

Bobbie Perkins, Co-Director Dallas Meditation Center, was an early reader providing honored suggestions and ideas.

My family:

Although my parents are both gone, they are with me every day. They raised me with an abundance of love. My father made me believe I could be and do anything I chose. My sweet mother taught me that all people are imperfect and yet worthy of unconditional love. Through the years I have learned that few are so blessed. Jake and Betty Muck were both wonderful examples of lives well-lived.

My brother, Dennis Muck, taught me nearly all I know about living a life filled with joy and happiness. He has always known how to live in the moment, whereas I had to learn it.

My husband, Lane King, is one of the gentlest and kindest men I have ever known. His love and support never waivers. Even through all the hours and angst of writing this book he was my most ardent supporter and encourager.

My cousin whom I call sister, Cindy Higgins, has shared her grief journey with me and been an inspiration along the way. She has also taught me that we can love and respect each other while seeing the world though different eyes.

Teachers:

My thanks would seem incomplete without mentioning all the teachers that have helped me grow and learn along the way. What an amazing profession, I can never thank them adequately!

That includes the authors of all the of books I have read. What an amazing world we live in, where the knowledge of the ages is so readily available. May that wealth of knowledge bless humanity and shine a light on the higher road.

Suggested Resources

The following books and digital resources have influenced my life and especially the writing of this book. If they are here, I have returned to them time and again to learn and better understand life, grief and death. I've listed them here for those who might want more resources to support their healing journey. They are not arranged in any specific priority scheme but grouped by topic. I believe all of them, and many more, should be easy to find via an internet search.

I'm always looking for more mind-expanding reads. Please let me know if you have favorites! I would love to check them out!

LOSS and GRIEF BOOKS

How to Survive the Loss of a Love by Melba Colgrove, Harold H. Bloomfield, and Peter McWilliams

Since the late 1970s this is the book I am most likely to give a friend experiencing loss. Maybe my favorite book on loss and grief and surviving.

The last Lecture by Randy Pausch

An amazing book, written about the last lecture a Carnegie Mellon Professor gave while dying from pancreatic cancer. It is full of joy and heartache and wisdom.

A Grief Observed by C.S. Lewis

A very personal journal written during the authors grief over the loss of his wife. It deals with the anguish of loss, rage, doubts and anger as he finds his path back to living.

When Bad Things Happen to Good People by Harold S. Hushner

The book that taught me about suffering and surviving and releasing guilt and anger.

How Can It Be All Right When Everything is All Wrong? By Lewis B. Smedes

A book about JOY found through grace.

It Was on Fire When I Lay down on It by Robert Fulgham

A great read about getting through troubling times.

No Mud, No Lotus by Thich Nhat Hanh

A great action book that helps one turn the mud of grief, uncertainty and change into the lotus flower of happiness.

The Grief Recovery Handbook by John W. James and Russell Friedman

A very practical and useful book on grief recovery. If I had found it before I wrote this book, I may not have written mine.

Self-Compassion by Kristin Neff

An amazing manual about taking care of yourself. She is the leading researcher on self-compassion; also see her website.

Don't Sweat the Small Stuff ... and It's All Small Stuff by Richard Carlson

A great help for processing through all the stresses of life.

Freddie the Leaf by Leo Buscaglia

A wonderful book that is equally meaningful and helpful for adults and children.

Talking about Death by Earl A. Grollman

A wonderful resource for helping children deal with loss, death and grief.

Liberating Losses by Jennifer Elison, Chris McGonigle

Some losses are liberating and bring relief. This book shines a light for the bereaved who experience relief and liberation after a death.

SPIRITUAL and LIFE PHILOSOPHY BOOKS
(Because dealing with Loss and Death always seem to end up tied to our spiritual beliefs and life philosophy.)

The Bible

This is where all my spiritual knowledge and life philosophy began back at the Christian Church in Downs, Kansas. I wouldn't change a thing about that wonderful church or the mind-expanding summer church camps I attended. They both supported my becoming a seeker of spiritual truths - wherever they might be found.

Unconditional Love by John Powell, S.J.

An in-depth look at unconditional love as the ultimate and highest goal to which a person can aspire.

The Prophet by Kahlil Gibran

A classic that still brings understanding. On death: "For life and death are one, even as the river and the sea are one."

Living Beautifully with Uncertainty and Change by Pema Chodron

There is almost nothing more painful and difficult than the uncertainty and change we experience when a loved one departs or dies. This book teaches a way to live with the impermanence and ever-shifting nature of life.

IS by Faith Freed

A spiritually eclectic book. Filled with love and wonder and joy and fresh spiritual thoughts.

Tao Te Ching (The Book of the Way) By Lao Tzu, interpretation by Stephen Mitchel

An ancient classic. Be sure to get the Stephen Mitchel interpretation. His translation is current, beautiful and meaningful in today's world. Simple truths translated into accessible English.

The Tao of Pooh by Benjamin Hoff
A funny and playful book that ties the essence of Winnie the Pooh to the depth of The Tao (the art or skill of doing something in harmony with the essential nature of the thing).

The Zen of Oz by Joey Green
A wonderful fun read with lots of great Zen insights from Oz.

The Four Agreements by Don Miguel Ruiz
A thoughtful vision of the world and how to be your best self in it. The life view is based on ancient Toltec knowledge and resonates with universal truth.

Living a Life of Awareness by Don Miguel Ruiz, JR.
A wonderful collection of daily meditations on the Toltec path.

Getting to Where You Are by Steven Harrison
An amazing book that I found extremely meaningful. In one of the margins I wrote: "I have lost my BELIEFS and gained my FAITH". Please don't read this if you are not ready or willing to re-examine and re-consider the truth of your beliefs.

Zen Mind, Beginner's Mind by Shunryu Suzuki
My first exposure to eastern philosophy and a classic.

The Power of NOW by Eckhart Tolle
The right book at the right time to change the course of my life.

The Wise Heart by Jack Kornfield
A powerful bedside book, to be referenced over and over again. Too much info to be absorbed in a single reading.

The Universe in a Single Atom by his holiness the Dalai Lama
An amazing merging of science and faith into a complete and

holy view of all that is.

PERSONAL GROWTH BOOKS

If Life is a Game, These are the Rules by Cherie Carter-Scott, Ph.D.

Author of The Ten Rules for Being Human. Life would have been easier if I had found this book when I was younger! An easy great read.

Life is Short - Wear Your Party Pants by Loretta LaRoche

One of my favorite books to give folks. A fun read that outlines ten simple truths that help create a joyful life.

Living Juicy by Sark

Creative, joyful and quirky daily morsels with amazing depth. Pure joy to read! A favorite of mine since 1996. Especially great for creative folks (and geez I think everyone is creative in some way).

Random Acts of Kindness by The Editors of Conari Press

A book of short clips appropriate for daily readings. It is a compilation of random act stories that will warm your heart and make you proud to be human. Reading it will make you want to join the Random Acts of Kindness movement started by Anne Herbert.

Live Boldly by Mary Anne Radmacher

A book that helps you open up your life, live without fear of judgement and become who you truly are. This book frees your heart and mind to live your highest dreams, become your best self, become who you were born to be and experience living free.

Inner Simplicity by Elaine St. James

A simple easy read which is set up to be daily meditation/reading friendly. She also wrote Simplify Your Life. Both are enriching and nourishing books to make your life better.

Hope for the Flowers by Trina Paulus
A wonderful story about hope.

Making Peace with Yourself by Harold H. Bloomfield, M.D. with Leonard Felder, Ph.D.
Enough said.

The Happiness Project by Gretchen Rubin
An amazing book that started Happiness Project Groups across the nation. The group I joined still informs my life and decisions today! Thank you Dorayne Breedlove and Dallas CSL!

Happy for No Reason by Marci Shimoff
More information and research than can be absorbed with one reading. I might even say - if you can only read one book on this list ... this might be it!

APPS FOR MINDFULNESS OR MEDITATION

CALM application. Free trials and specials available.
www.calm.com

HEADSPACE application. Free trials and specials available.
www.Headspace.com

WEBSITES

NATIONAL HOSPICE AND PALLIATIVE CARE ORGANIZATION provides resources for families and care providers.
www.nhpco.org

COMPASSIONATE FRIENDS an organization to support those

grieving the loss of a child.
www.centering.org

CENTERING CORPORATION provides bereavement resources for those experiencing grief.
www.compassionatefriends.org

SELF-COMPASSION site by Dr. Kristin Neff, the leading self-compassion researcher.
www.self-compassion.org

DALLAS MEDITATION CENTER The meditation center where I practice weekly.
www.dallasmeditationcenter.com

GREATER GOOD SCIENCE CENTER provides amazing resources for improving our relationships and our experience with life.
www.ggsc.berkeley.edu

CHARTER FOR COMPASSION provides insights into living a compassionate life.
www.charterforcompassion.org

Photo: Cheryl Muck

Photo: Cheryl Muck

www.ingramcontent.com/pod-product-compliance
Lightning Source LLC
Chambersburg PA
CBHW071215090426
42736CB00014B/2840

* 9 7 8 0 5 7 8 7 5 1 9 6 2 *